# Divorce Planning

A Step-by-Step Guide to Navigating
Through Your Divorce

# Divorce Planning

A Step-by-Step Guide to Navigating
Through Your Divorce

Laurie B. Giles, JD

Prospering Leaf Press

WHAT NOW? DIVORCE PLANNING
A Step-By-Step Guide to Navigating Through Your Divorce by Laurie Giles, JD
Prospering Leaf Press
Concord, NC 28027

The publisher expressly states that no specific legal or financial advice is contained in this book, and that the reader should retain professional legal or financial counsel regarding specific questions and issues.

Library of Congress Cataloging-in-Publication Data
Giles, Laurie.
WHAT NOW? DIVORCE PLANNING
A Step-By-Step Guide to Navigating Through Your Divorce / Laurie Giles.
p.cm.
ISBN: 978-0-9825661-0-7

TThis book is dedicated to the memory of Joanne and Laura, two extraordinary women whose struggles with their divorces and the aftermath forever changed my views on how to more effectively help women through this transition. You inspired me to write this book.

# Table of Contents

# STEP THREE: YOUR NEEDS AND WANTS

## STEP FOUR: PUTTING YOUR PLAN INTO ACTION

# STEP ONE

## Laying the Foundation

# *Chapter 1*

## *What Now? Tactical Divorce Planning*

*Tricia Hart had always been a very outgoing fun loving person, a real social butterfly. She enjoyed spending time with friends and family, always the life of the party. Her husband, Brad, loathed socializing. He often refused to accompany Tricia to social events and family gatherings. Brad's idea of a good time was a bowl of chips and a beer in front of a mammoth size television watching anything related to sports for hours on end. As the years went on their differences caused great acrimony in their relationship. They argued bitterly. The arguments extended to include many other issues; money, intimacy and household chores. Their arguing intensified and they were arguing nearly every day. Finally after 17 years, Tricia was done being incredibly unhappy. On January 1, 2006, Tricia made a New Year's resolution; she was going to file for divorce.*

*After surfing the internet for a few minutes, Tricia located an attorney and scheduled a consultation with him. The attorney convinced her that he was the best attorney to handle her divorce, and that there was no need to check out other attorneys. Convinced by his sales pitch, Tricia handed over a $7,500.00 retainer. She gave him a single directive, "I want the house!"*

*The attorney never asked her if she could afford the house or if the title was clear. He failed to inquire about her needs and wants for her post divorce life. Five months into the process, her attorney telephoned to tell her that he had just struck a great settlement deal for her. He told her that if she came into the office that day and signed the agreement the divorce could be final almost immediately. When she got to the office, she took fifteen minutes to look over* the agreement. The agreement stated that Tricia would get the house; she was to be responsible for paying the mortgage, taxes and homeowner insurance. In addition she would receive $14, 000.00 in cash, and $700.00 per month alimony for 8 years. Pursuant to the agreement, Brad would receive the household furnishings and $75,000.00 in cash. He also retained 100% of his pension. Tricia was thrilled. Her attorney had negotiated what she believed was a great deal. She got the one thing she wanted . . . the house. Wanting to end the process as soon as possible, Tricia made a rash, impetuous decision and signed the final agreement.

Tricia quickly found that her salary did not cover the mortgage, taxes, insurance and other living expenses, but she was able to squeak by with the alimony she was receiving.

One year later, Brad lost his job. He was able to have the divorce agreement modified, suspending his alimony obligation until he was able to secure employment.

Unable to make the mortgage payments without the alimony, Tricia attempted to refinance the house. Much to her shock and dismay, the property had numerous liens due to an unresolved civil judgment and non payment of federal taxes. The refinance was denied. Tricia was left with no alternative but to sell the house. Because of the liens and encumbrances, as well as a down real estate market, the house was sold at a loss.

Tricia had spent the entire $14, 000 cash settlement redecorating the house. With no money to start over, she was in a real bind. If Tricia had taken the time to develop a plan, she would have realized the 'great' deal was in reality a horrible deal.

Many people, women in particular, frequently approach divorce in the same manner in which they approach a department store clearance sale. Anxious to find a great deal, they grab anything that looks like it might fit, particularly if the price is right. Caught up in the excitement of getting a bargain, they fail to give any real consideration as to whether or not the purchase is truly a good deal. Later, inspecting the purchase away from the sale excitement, it becomes clear the deal was not as good as it appeared. With clarity of thought, the tear or stain becomes noticeable. Trying on the garment, it becomes obvious that it does not fit properly; it looks awful. Purchasing the garment was definitely the wrong decision. All is not lost. Simply return the item to the store and exchange it for something more appropriate or get a full refund.

Sadly, many women approach their divorce process the same way. They retain a lawyer that talks a good game, they make rash decisions in the emotional heat of the moment, and then agree to terms which do not make financial or legal sense just to get the process over. But, unlike the clearance sale find, divorce agreements are not so easily taken back. You will be legally bound by the decisions you make for a very long time. Generally, in order to have an agreement legally modified or amended, there must be a showing of a substantial change in circumstances.

By developing a tactical plan of approach you will gain the knowledge and understanding to be able to separate good deals from bad deals. While divorce is never easy, it does not need to destroy you or your family. Acting with calm and clarity of thought will serve you much better in making rational appropriate decisions which will work for you in the long run.

Divorce, as you may suspect or already realize, is difficult and fraught with stress and emotional upheaval. The process is daunting and overwhelming. In most cases there are two components of divorce: emotional and legal. These components happen concurrently. Because it is difficult to deal with the emotional aspects and the legal practicalities at the same time, many women tend to address one but not the other. Frequently, the emotional aspects - the hurt, pain and anger - receive first priority, leaving legal aspects to chance. This is a colossal mistake. Emotions will evolve and change over time. However, legally binding agreements will be in effect for a very long time.

In order to emerge successfully, and in a good place to begin your new post divorce life, a solid proactive plan of approach must be developed. By taking the time and putting in the effort to develop a plan tailored to your individual circumstances, you ensure that the actions you take and the decisions you make during your divorce process will be well thought out.

**There are many benefits to taking a proactive tactical approach to divorce from both legal and emotional stand points. Benefits include:**

- Reduce attorney fees.
- Decrease stress.
- Diminish acrimony.
- Maintain greater control over the legal process.
- Control your future.
- Act proactively not reactively.
- Set the stage for making sound rational decisions.
- Establish negotiation and settlement goals and parameters.

## ~~Goals~~

When prepared correctly, your *What Now? Tactical Divorce Plan* will accomplish seven major goals:

1. Develop the right personal and professional teams to help you get through the process and on with your life.
2. Understand your current financial, legal and health conditions.
3. Crystallize your current wishes and needs.
4. Figure out your future wishes and needs.
5. Facilitate the shift from couple mindset to single mindset life management.
6. Plan how to reach a settlement that meets your needs and wants.
7. Set the foundation to create the life you desire.

## ~~Planning Steps~~

There are four steps in completing your *What Now? Tactical Divorce Plan*.

### Step One: Laying the Foundation

During step one, you will take the first steps to get through the divorce process, find your inner strength, and begin to put your professional and personal team together.

### Step Two: Understanding the Here and Now

Step two guides you through ascertaining your current legal, financial and medical conditions and needs. You will understand and evaluate what is best for your children.

## Step Three: Your Needs and Wants

During step three, you will determine what you need and want legally, financially and emotionally for your future. You will create a custody and co-parenting plan.

## Step Four: Putting Your Plan Into Action

Step four puts your plan into action. During this step, you will reach settlement or get through trial, and redefine yourself to live the life you deserve.

The steps build on one another and they should be completed sequentially.

# *Chapter 2*

## *What Now? Getting Geared Up*

### ~~Taking Action~~

An overwhelming majority of marriages that fail do not fail overnight or over one incident. Generally, the divorce decision is a long time in coming and the result of a culmination of numerous problems. Divorce is never the first option; however, in some instances, it is the only viable option. When you decide it is time to divorce or you are served with divorce papers by your soon to be ex-husband, emotions will likely kick into high gear, and may run the gambit from anger to despair. It is likely that you may feel overburdened and overwhelmed.

Many women wrongly believe that contacting a lawyer is the logical first action step to take. In reality this is the most illogical first step. Stepping back and taking stock of where you are emotionally should be your first action step. It is virtually impossible to make sound rational decisions and move forward when overwhelmed by emotions. You must get your emotions in check before moving forward with the divorce process.

## Some Common Emotions and Feelings:

- Fear
- Hurt
- Anger
- Despair
- Relief
- Grief
- Overburdened
- Frustration

## ~~Finding Your Inner Strength and Courage~~

Divorce is going to be tough, perhaps one of the toughest times of your life, but you can and will get through. Finding your inner strength and courage is pivotal to getting through successfully. There are countless ways to find inner strength and courage.

## Some Ideas to Consider Are:

- Prayer
- Meditation
- Repeat a daily mantra
- Join a support group
- Journaling
- Develop a personal vision statement
- Develop a personal vision board
- Exercise
- Read self help books
- Participate in counseling
- Take a personal retreat

Whatever has worked for you in the past during tough times may well work again. Give it a try.

## ~~Know Your Rights and Options~~

Would you ever attempt to prepare a new dish without some initial preparation? Of course you wouldn't. At the very least reading the recipe in order to understand the cooking method is a must. Engaging in any unfamiliar task, sport or job without first understanding the fundamentals would be imprudent. Why then would anyone start a divorce process without an understanding of the basics?

Unfortunately, many women fail to acquire a basic understanding of the divorce process. Many fail to learn about their options and rights. An educated consumer is a wise consumer. Be wise; become knowledgeable about your rights and options. Learn as much about the process as possible. Divorce laws are state specific. Learn what your rights and options are in the state in which you live. Check your state's judicial website and court library to obtain available information. Read the laws pertaining to procedural aspects of divorce and those specifically pertaining to your issues. Check with the local bar association regarding any available resources. Many law firm web sites offer locale specific educational resources. Visit the court house where your divorce will be heard. Speak to the court clerk. If allowable, observe actual divorce proceedings. In short, get a feel of the landscape. Learn as much about the process and your rights as possible. The more information you have, the better equipped you will be to take appropriate actions and make sound decisions.

# *Chapter 3*

## *Sharing the News*

*To the outside world Liz and Greg seemed to have the perfect marriage. They had a beautiful home and three wonderful children. When they attended their children's school functions and games, the two always appeared extremely loving and happy. But inside of the house things were diametrically different. Liz and Greg had barely spoken for months, and when they did it was limited to talking about the kids, bills or needed house repairs. They argued almost daily. They had not been intimate for over a year. Liz was miserable. Deciding that divorce was her only option, she began the process.*

*Liz confided in her sister, Roberta, who lived in Europe, that the hardest part was feeling alone. Liz had not told anyone about the impending divorce but desperately wanted a friend to talk to. Roberta suggested that Liz make a list of her closest friends and start sharing the news with them one by one. Roberta told her that by the time she reached her fourth friend Liz would feel much more comfortable. Taking her sister's advice, Liz began sharing the news with her close friends. To her pleasant surprise, it worked. By her third telephone call she was comfortable enough to start letting her friends in. Liz developed a network of friends who she could lean on.*

Often opening up and sharing personal information can be challenging. However, in the course of divorce it is usually helpful to have people to confide in.

## ~~Developing Your Personal Support Network~~

Before you start confiding in anyone and developing a personal support network, take a mental inventory of the people in your life. Ask yourself who among those people should be confided in and who should not?

Many women have one or two very close friends with whom they share everything. For these women developing a personal support system is simple. It's already in place.

Some women have several close friends who play different roles in their lives. If you fall into this second group, decide who will be in your support circle by taking stock of your friends and their roles in your life. Who should and can help you during what is going to be a very challenging time? There are many types of roles friends play. Among them are:

Good time friend:    fun to spend time with, but not necessarily a confidante.

Historic friend:    has been in your life long enough to help you look at things from a historic point of view.

Logical friend:    thinks logically and will keep you focused on the logic of your actions.

Reality check friend: clearly points out the truth of the matter, no holds barred.

Cheerleader friend:    unabashedly supportive and
                       will cheer you on.

It is important to be mindful of the individualized role of each of your friends. Don't expect them to act outside of the established relational role. Your reality check friend is not going to just blindly support you; don't get upset if she questions your actions. By the same token, don't expect your cheerleader friend to let you know when you are being unreasonable.  It just is not the nature of the relationship.

Many of us have people in our lives with whom we share a cordial friendship - situational friends. These are the people with whom there is an acquaintance because of a particular situation: work, fellow church members, the other team moms, or the neighbor down the street.  Often these are the people with whom we spend the greatest amount of time. But, when it comes to friendship, time spent does not necessarily translate into closeness.

You may have some friends with whom you may want to limit your sharing:  the always negative person, the overly judgmental person and the know-it-all person.  Confiding in such people may serve to cloud your judgment and exacerbate your stress level.

## Male Friends

Many divorcing women wonder about the role of male friends in their personal support network. Divorce can become contentious. Do not add fuel to the fire by developing retaliatory friendships or with the intent of hurting or enraging your soon to be ex-husband. A good rule of thumb is to maintain status quo when it comes to opposite sex friendships. Maintain those which have been long standing and platonic. Stay away from developing new opposite sex friendships as they may have the proclivity to have the appearance of impropriety.

## Who Should Not Be in Your Inner Circle?

Unless you share a very close relationship beyond your role as in-law, including his parents or siblings or other relatives in your inner circle is probably unwise. It is also unfair to put them in the middle. In short, unless an issue directly affects your physical safety or the physical or emotional safety of your children, leave the in-laws out.

Your husband's employer and co-workers should not be in your inner circle. Nor should they be sought after allies. While it may be vindicating to play victim or make him look bad, damaging his career and jeopardizing his ability to earn income will hurt you and your children in the long run.

## ~~Broaching the Subject with Your Inner Circle~~

Sharing personal news with friends and family can be stressful and emotional. This often holds true when sharing the news that you are getting divorced. For some women divorce is embarrassing. Others feel divorce is an admission of failure. For some the divorce decision leads them to become fearful of rejection by family or friends.

To alleviate the difficulty, many women develop an informal or formal plan of how and with whom to discuss their divorce. Be cautious as to what information you share. Once information is out it can not be retracted.

## 5 Tips for Broaching the Subject

1. Tell the people with whom you are most comfortable first.
2. Share the news when you are ready.
3. Plan ahead what information you will share.
4. Don't feel obligated to share information you do not wish to share.
5. Prepare for both positive and negative reactions and be ready to deal with them.

## ~~Who Else Should Be Told About Your Divorce?~~

There may be additional people who should be told about your impending divorce.

**School faculty, staff and administrators:** If your children are not yet in high school, it may be advisable to let those who work directly with your children know about your impending divorce. That does not mean you have to tell everyone from the school bus driver to the assistant coach. Limit the dissemination of information to those administrators, faculty and staff members who are directly involved with your child. Do not attempt to get teachers and other school personnel to become your allies. This not only places them in an awkward position, but it has no place in your personal divorce. It is unnecessary and inappropriate to discuss non child related issues with school officials.

If your children are upper middle school or high school age, telling teachers and coaches of the changing home situation is far less important. Generally, telling school personnel can be limited to an as-needed basis.

**Employers:** Many divorcing people wonder if they should tell their employer about the divorce. Two pivotal areas to consider when deciding whether to inform your employer are 1) your relationship with your employer and 2) your rationale for discussing the information.

If you are unsure how to handle this conversation, perhaps discussing your workplace environment with a trusted co-worker will prove helpful. Should you decide to share the information, discuss it from the employer's standpoint. This might including discussing how your divorce process will or will not affect your employment: time-off or a need for flexibility of hours. Do not imply that your performance or productivity will be affected by the divorce. Regardless of how much you believe your employer values you, they are still in business and must put business needs first. Also consider if it will affect your career if your co-workers believe you are distracted and perhaps off your game. At some point you may need to have a discussion with human resources regarding benefits and other changes.

## ~~Dealing With Unsolicited Advice, Hurtful Comments and Thoughtless Questions~~

Everyone from your mother to the neighbor down the street will have tons of advice. People will ask inappropriate questions and make hurtful comments. Be prepared to handle such advice and comments with grace and dignity. Consider these responses:

Unsolicited advice: When my cousin got divorced, her lawyer told her to . . . . . . .
*Thank you; I will give that information some thought.*

Question: What happened?
*Are you really interested in hearing the gory details?*

Comment: I bet he cheated on you.
*Why would you think that? Were you in that situation?*

Question: Did he leave you for a younger woman?
*You should ask him that.*

Comment/Question: Your husband is such a great guy; are you sure you want to give him up?
*Oh, I didn't realize you were so familiar with my husband?*

Comment: Divorce is against our religion.
*I would like to look that up in the Bible (or Koran or Torah); is that in the same scripture as 'do not judge'?*

Remember, take the high road. Maintain your grace and dignity.

# *Chapter 4*

## *Your Professional Team*

Divorce has many components, including legal, emotional, and financial. You need a team of professionals who can individually and collectively address all of the components of your divorce. Hiring professionals in each area will help you to approach divorce in a comprehensive manner.

### ~~Team Players~~

Decide which professionals you need on your team to best effectuate your goals. Your team may include any or all of the following professional members:

- Therapist/counselor
- Life/transition coach
- Physician
- Accountant
- Asset valuator
- Financial planner
- Attorney

## ~~Understanding Player Roles and Responsibilities~~

Therapist:    assists you in working through the emotional aspects of divorce. A good therapist will also help you to understand and work through your emotions, perceptions and barriers.

Life/Transition
Coach:    guides you through the transition and helps you create your post divorce life. Be very cautious not to confuse life coaching with therapy. Unless your life coach is also a trained licensed mental health professional, therapy or psychological counseling should not be given.

Physician:    diagnoses and treats your physical condition.

Accountant:    advises as to personal state and federal tax implications and consequences. Accountants may also address sale or liquidation of the business for business owners.

Asset Valuator(s):    ascertains the value of property including real estate, jewelry, art, antiques, businesses and pensions.

Financial
Planner/Advisor:    develops and implements a strategy to meet financial goals and needs.

Attorney:    represents  legal interest and resolves legal issues.

## ~~Choosing the Right Team~~

There are numerous methods of locating professionals. Some sources to consider are the internet, friends, and referral services. Often other professionals can be a great source for referrals to professionals with whom they have a working relationship.

With some professionals, particularly attorneys, it is a good idea to watch them in action. I have seen many people sit in the back of a court room and just observe. This is a great way to find out the actual working style as well as the rapport between the attorney and their colleagues and court staff, particularly the judge.

Once you have located prospective professionals, the next step is to choose the right professionals for you. The best way to find the best professional for you is to interview each prospect. Interview as many prospective professionals as necessary, until you believe you have found a good fit. Most reputable professionals offer consultations prior to engagement.

Use the three C's as a guidepost.

### ~~The Three C's~~

1. Competency - is the professional competent to handle your matter?
2. Comfort - are you comfortable with the professional?
3. Cost - is the cost of service affordable and doable?

## Questions to Ask During the Initial Consultation

### Eight questions to ask prospective therapists:
1. What professional training and education have they had?
2. How long have they been in practice?
3. What professional licenses do they hold?
4. What experience do they have working with divorce cases?
5. If necessary, will they be amenable to testifying in court? If so, what is the fee?
6. What is the fee for services?
7. Do they accept insurance?
8. Are they willing to work collaboratively with other team members?

### Seven questions to ask prospective life coaches:
1. What professional training have they had?
2. How long have they been in practice?
3. Do they have experience working with divorce cases?
4. What is the fee for services?
5. How are sessions provided? In person, via telephone?
6. What is the general coaching philosophy?
7. Are they willing to work collaboratively with other team members?

### Nine questions to ask perspective physicians:
1. What are the areas of specialty?
2. What education and training did they receive?
3. Are there any pending malpractice actions?
4. Have there been any past disciplinary actions by the

medical board?

5. How long have they been in practice?
6. What are the service fees?
7. Which insurance do they accept?
8. How are co-pays and other out of pocket costs handled?
9. At which hospitals do they hold privileges?

## Eight questions to ask perspective accountants:

1. Are they experienced in working with divorce cases?
2. How long have they been in practice?
3. What are their billing practices?
4. If necessary, will they testify in court; if so, what are the fees for court testimony?
5. If necessary will they participate in settlement negotiations? If so, what is the cost?
6. Are they a licensed CPA? If so, is the license in good standing?
7. Are they willing to work collaboratively with other team members?
8. Are there any pending malpractice or disciplinary actions?

## Six questions to ask perspective asset valuators:

1. What type of experience do they have?
2. What are their certifications/licensing?
3. What is the cost of valuations?
4. Have they ever given court testimony?
5. Are they willing to testify in court if necessary? If so, what is the associated cost?
6. Are they willing to work collaboratively with other team members?

## Eight questions to ask perspective financial planners/ advisors:

1. How long have they been in practice?
2. What certifications are held?
3. What is the divorce specific experience?
4. What is the cost for services?
5. If necessary, will they participate in settlement negotiations? If so, what is the cost?
6. If necessary, will they testify in court; if so, what are the fees for court testimony?
7. What is the fee structure?
8. Are they willing to work collaboratively with other team members?

## Nine questions to ask prospective attorneys:

1. How much experience do they have with divorce cases?
2. How long have they been in practice?
3. What is the hourly billing rate?
4. How much is the upfront retainer?
5. What additional fees are charged? (i.e. copies, court fees, service of process)
6. What is their general approach to divorce cases?
7. Are they licensed by the state bar? If so, is the license in good standing?
8. Are there any pending malpractice or disciplinary actions?
9. Are they willing to work collaboratively with other team members?

## Some Do's and Don'ts to Consider:

### Do

- Research the experience, practice methods and approach.
- Use the rule of three; consult with at least three professionals.
- Check the licensing board to see if there is a history of repeated disciplinary actions.
- Be cautious of a professional who is reluctant to offer a consultation or unwilling to answer interview questions.

### Don't

- Be swayed by flashy advertisements, there may not be any correlation with the ability and competence of the professional.
- Select a professional based on reputation of being contentious or underhanded.
- Retain a professional with whom you are not comfortable.
- Be afraid to ask questions.

## Step One Summary

Often the hardest step is the initial step. This is certainly true of What Now? Divorce Planning. Facing the end of a marriage is always emotionally challenging. Taking affirmative steps to move forward is even more challenging. Congratulations! You got through it.

**The goals of step one which should have been achieved are:**

1. Found the inner strength and courage to face the divorce head on.
2. Established your personal support network.
3. Chosen your professional team.
4. Laid the groundwork for completing the remainder of the *What Now? Divorce Plan.*

# STEP TWO

## Understanding the Here and Now

# *Chapter Five*

## *Financial*

In order to effectively plan for the future as well as live prudently in the present, knowing your true financial position is critical. For long term planning purposes a cursory understanding of your financial state is insufficient. Delve as deeply as possible.

### ~~Day to Day Finances~~

Begin by ascertaining day-to-day financial management. Figure out the total household income: how much money comes in. Then figure out household expenses: the money that goes out to pay bills.

### Income

Many couples receive income from multiple income streams.

First consider consistent income sources. Consistent income is received on a regular basis in a specific amount and is derived most frequently from employment and retirement benefits which are in pay status.

Next consider variable income, which varies as to amount and frequency of receipt. Categories of income considered as variable income include self employment income, part time home based sales, business income, partnership draws, tips, commissions, bonuses and residual income.

Income derived from income producing assets can be considered either consistent or variable depending on the specific asset.

**Income from employment:** pay received as a result of work performed: wages and salaries.

**Retirement income:** funds received from pensions and other retirement benefits in pay status. This includes annuities, 401(k), pensions and social security benefits received.

**Income-producing assets:** income derived from an asset in which the recipient is actively involved in the management or production of income. Business interest income and investment real estate income fall into this category.

**Passive income:** results from performance of an asset in which the recipient is not actively involved in the management or production of income. Stock dividends and bank interest are examples of passive income.

**Residual income**: is derived from previous work or efforts and could be royalties or renewal commissions from prior sales made of products or services, such as insurance and patents.

## Expenses

Household and personal expenses can be divided into two categories: fixed and variable.

**Variable expenses:** those expenses which fluctuate based upon consumption or usage. These include utilities, heating fuel, credit card payments, un-reimbursed medical expenses, food, clothing, property upkeep and auto repairs.

Variable expenses are calculated based upon average expenditure. Divide the total expenditure or payment made over the previous 12-month period by 12. This figure is the monthly average.

If you do not have access to monthly statements most utility companies, credit card companies, physicians and pharmacies are able and willing to provide a 12-month payment history.

**Fixed expenses:** expenses which require predetermined payments as to amount and due date. Mortgages, taxes, insurance premiums, rent and auto loans are considered fixed expenses. Because fixed expenses do not fluctuate they are calculated using the payment amount.

Once all expenses have been calculated, add 10%-20% to the final expense total in contemplation of cost of living increases as well as unexpected and miscellaneous expenses.

<u>Income – expenses = monthly personal</u>
household operating cost

## ~~Assets~~

Next determine assets and liabilities. Figure out what is owned and what is owed. In determining the division of assets and liabilities there will be a determination as to which  assets and liabilities are individual and which are joint or part of the marital estate. At this juncture determine all assets and liabilities to ascertain a full picture of the current situation.

**Assets:** are items expected to have a future value or benefit to the owner. Three types of assets should be considered: 1. intangible 2. tangible and 3. income producing.

**Intangible assets:** do not have a physical form but have an ascertainable value. Common listings among business owner's intangible assets may include knowledge, professional identity, goodwill and trade secrets.

**Tangible assets:** have a physical form, and ascertainable value. Equity in real estate, jewelry, art, collectibles, gold, silver, stock accounts, bonds and bank accounts are among items considered tangible assets.

**Income producing assets:** in addition to producing income, income producing assets have an ascertainable value. The total equity value of the asset, such as a rental property, should be considered in the inventorying of assets.

For example:

The total value of the property is $275,000.00
Balance of mortgage owed is $125,000.00

$275,000.00 - $125,000.00 = $150,000.00
Value   -   Mortgage balance   =   Equity

Value included in asset inventory = $150,000.00

## Asset Valuation

Having a clear understanding of not only what assets are owned but knowing the value of those assets is crucial to fully understand your current financial situation. Asset valuation is also necessary in developing a realistic plan for settlement negotiations. Should your divorce proceed to trial, knowing the true value of assets is a must.

Many people get into a quandary differentiating between items that are true assets and sentimental pieces. Items with mere sentimental value are not considered in the inventorying of assets because they do not hold future monetary value to the owner. In making the distinction ask yourself, is the asset of any value to anyone except you or your spouse? Would someone else purchase the item if you were to sell them?

## Valuing Assets

Prior to engaging the services of a professional asset valuator, spend some time doing a preliminary investigation in order to establish a baseline value. Attend local real estate open houses and browse antique shops and galleries. This preliminary work will also help distinguish between true assets and sentimental pieces.

There are numerous valuation methods which may be employed depending on asset type.

**Real estate:** nationally, the real estate market has been on a downward trend and in some markets a downward spiral. When having real estate valued given the current economic status, keep in mind the valuation may change dramatically over short periods of time.

Three methods of valuing real estate are generally accepted: market value, assessed value and appraised value.

**Market value:** established by a real estate agent who compares the property to similar properties in the area which have recently sold or are listed for sale. The value established is based upon reasonable sale price.

The greatest benefit of using this method is cost. Market analyses are often offered as a complimentary service by realtors. If a fee is charged, it is generally nominal ranging between $75.00 and $150.00.

The downside to using the market value method is that valuation is very general and dictated by market conditions and not the specific condition of the property. Market valuation relies solely on realtor opinion. Since opinions can differ greatly, obtain at least three reports and use either an average of the values given or the middle value.

For example:

> Agent one values the home at $460,000.00
> Agent two values the home at $496,000.00
> Agent three values the home at $473,000.00

> Use a value of $476,000.00 (average) or $473,000.00 (middle)

If unfamiliar with local realtors, contact the local real estate board for referrals.

**Assessed value:** is the value assigned by the municipal taxing authority in which the property is located to determine the amount of property tax due. The assessed value generally equals 65%-75% of market value. The percentage is determined most often by the state.

The upside of using the assessed value is that it is free to obtain. Simply contact the municipal taxing authority and request the assessed value or the applicable percentage.

The downside of using the assessed value method is the infrequency of reassessment. Depending on state statues, which vary from state to state, municipalities are only required to conduct property reassessments every three, five or more years. The valuation on record with the municipality may be outdated.

To determine market value of the property based upon the assessed value, ask the taxing authority what percentage has been utilized and divide the assessed value by the percentage.

For example:

Assessed value is $489.500.00
Percentage of market value is 70%
$489,500 divided by .70 = $699,285.00
Market value = $689,285.00

**Appraised value:** the most comprehensive and accurate real estate valuation method is conducted by a trained licensed appraiser who determines value based on property specifics. The appraiser physically investigates the property including condition of roofing, foundation, and workability of appliances. Inspection and testing of all systems including heating, cooling, electrical and plumbing is also conducted. The final report assigns value and details necessary repairs and upgrades.

In a majority of states, real estate appraisers are certified and licensed. If your state has such a requirement, be sure the appraiser hired holds a valid license and is certified.

In order to locate a qualified appraiser, check with local banks and real estate agencies for referrals. The cost of an appraisal generally ranges between $350-$800 depending upon location and size of property.

**Jewelry:** generally speaking gold, silver, and other precious metals and stones are valuated by utilizing published indexes or by a piece specific appraisal. Piece condition is pivotal to the valuation. Having an appraisal performed by a gemologist or jeweler will establish the most accurate value. Many jewelry retailers offer appraisal services. Check with the National Association of Jewelry Appraisers for referrals.

**Artwork:** is valued based upon a piece specific appraisal. Local art dealers, galleries and museums can provide referrals for art appraisers.

**Coin Collections:** the three most common valuation methods used to determine the value of rare and collectable coins are grading, published index and appraisal. Similar to jewelry the condition of a specific coin affects the value. It is wise to have coins professionally graded or appraised. If you are unfamiliar with the process check with a local coin dealer or coin collecting association for referrals.

**Antiques:** there are countless types of antiques. Physical condition of a given piece is pivotal in determining the value of the piece. The values of similar pieces may vary greatly. It is recommended pieces be appraised by a professional antique appraiser. Obtain referrals for reputable antique appraisers by checking with local dealers who deal with the specific type of item.

**Securities:** stocks, bonds, mutual funds and other securities are perhaps the easiest assets to valuate. Values are posted in the financial section of newspapers as well as online. Review these sources to obtain a value. For more complex investment accounts, contact a broker.

### Liquid Assets

Liquid assets are assets which are in a cash form or easily convertible to cash. Among these assets are bank accounts, stocks, bonds, mutual funds and other securities.

Liquid assets are perhaps the easiest assets to valuate. Values are posted in the financial section of newspapers as well as online. Review these sources to obtain a value. For more complex investment accounts, contact the broker.

## ~~Liabilities~~

Liabilities result out of borrowing funds to purchase goods or services: credit cards, car notes, mortgages, and home equity lines of credit. Repayment in full of liabilities is conditioned on the occurrence of a specific event such as sale or liquidation of the asset or failure to make installment payments.

Liabilities are calculated based upon total amount of indebtedness. Determine the amount of liability by calculating the entire balance due.

It is not uncommon for couples to receive financial assistance from family and friends. Often the money is considered a gift. However, if there is an expectation of repayment, be sure to include the sum due in your liability calculation.

Assets - Liabilities = Net Worth

## ~~Tax Issues~~

Frequently state and federal tax issues are a major point of contention during divorce. You must ascertain your tax situation. Even if you believe you are aware of the details of prior tax filings, obtain copies from the IRS as well as from your state income tax agency to be sure the filing matches what you believe. Secondly, as a precautionary measure contact both agencies to be sure there are no outstanding tax issues which you are not aware of. It is far better to uncover this information and deal with any tax issues now than to be surprised with a tax bill after the divorce is final.

# *Chapter 6*

## *Legal*

Colleen and Greg, who met during college, married 3 weeks after graduation. They have two children, Jillian, aged 15 and Greg Jr., aged 11. During the marriage, Colleen was employed as an engineer for a Fortune 500 company. Greg was self employed as an IT consultant. In their day-to-day financial management, each retains separate bank accounts. They divide the payment of household expenses. They also have two joint credit cards which are used to pay necessary expenses. Colleen's $76,000 annual salary is used to pay household utilities, food, homeowner's insurance and auto insurance, children's activities and family vacations and entertainment. Greg, whose business generates an average annual income of $125,000.00, is responsible for the payment of the home mortgage, auto loans, the two joint credit cards and property taxes.

The couple lived what Colleen believed to be a very comfortable life. She also believed that Greg was paying the bills that he was responsible for. One day Colleen attempted to utilize one of the joint credit cards to purchase school supplies for the children. The card was declined. She then attempted to utilize the other card, and it too was declined. She was positive there must be an error, but telephoned both of the credit card companies just to be sure. The first representative advised her that the card was 60 days past due and purchases could not be made. The second representative advised her that the card had been canceled because it was 3 months delinquent. When she questioned Greg about this he assured her it was an oversight, and that he would make the payment immediately. She had no idea that his business was *failing, and not generating anywhere near enough income to pay his portion of the bills. Over the next several months similar situations happened, causing Colleen to become irate. The couple began having disagreements over finances. Finally the mortgage holder telephoned regarding late mortgage payments. Colleen was furious and decided to obtain a credit report to find out exactly what was going on. She was horrified to discover that she had a very poor credit rating which included numerous late payments and charge-offs. She also discovered two outstanding judgments for unpaid accounts. She didn't have knowledge of many of the accounts. Feeling betrayed, she filed for divorce.*

Scenarios similar to that of Colleen and Greg are very common. Many people, women in particular, do not find out about outstanding legal issues until the divorce process begins. Many do not discover legal problems until after the divorce is final. It is crucial to take a careful look at your current legal situation prior to the divorce process.

## ~~Lawsuits, Judgments, and Liens~~

In a majority of states a court entered judgment is enforceable for a minimum of 10 years. In most states, creditors holding civil judgments can request renewal of a judgment to extend time for enforceability. If the request for renewal is granted by a court, the judgment may be collectible for 20 or more years. Remember, just because a judgment no longer appears on a credit report does not mean the debt goes away. For a variety of reasons, many spouses are unaware of outstanding judgments. Even if you believe that this does not hold true in your personal situation, check court and public records to see if there is any record of pending court actions or outstanding judgments.

**Property liens:** the existence of liens or other encumbrances filed against real estate will affect the ability to sell or mortgage the property. This is very important in divorce, as often one party obtains a mortgage to buy out the other's interest in the house. If the house is to be sold as part of the divorce settlement, the existence of liens will affect the sale. Creditors or service providers may file a property lien without the knowledge or understanding of the owner.

Frequently, once a home mortgage is paid, the lender sends a document known as a release directly to the borrower. The release is documented evidence that the debt has been paid in full. Borrowers should send the release to the municipality for recording on the land records. Many borrowers unknowingly put the document away for safe keeping, and fail to send it to the municipality. The lien continues to appear as an encumbrance until the release is recorded.

A title search will reveal the existence of any liens or encumbrances which have been filed. Have a title search performed to be sure there are no liens filed against the property. Contact a local title search firm to have the search performed. The fee generally ranges between $250 and $650.00 depending upon location and complexity of the search.

### ~~Credit~~

It can not be reiterated enough - your credit standing can and will effect your future dramatically. Your credit rating can be directly tied to your ability to move forward, purchase a new home, secure a rental, or obtain credit. You must know your current status prior to embarking upon the divorce process. If you have not had a credit check run in the last 30 days, immediately have one run. While 30 days may seem like a very short period of time, marital problems often lead to non payment of bills, which will lead to a negative credit rating. It is advisable to obtain your credit report intermittently during your divorce process. This is not a suggestion, it is a directive. Do it.

## ~~Legal Ties~~

**Entangled legally with others:** Co-signing loans for friends and relatives is not uncommon. Get the current status of any loans for which you and/or your spouse are co-signers. Often misunderstood is the liability of co-signers. Co-signers share legal responsibility for the payment of debt equally with the primary borrower. It is imperative that your attorney and financial team members are made aware of any such loans.

If a friend or family member has co-signed a loan for you and your spouse, be sure to inform them of the impending divorce, so they may protect their legal rights' interest.

# *Chapter 7*

## *Medical*

After 23 years of marriage, 54 year old Nancy still believed she was married to the man of her dreams; her knight in shining armor. She thought the marriage would last forever. One day, Brian came home from work and announced that he was miserable and wanted out of the marriage. Nancy was devastated. Although she was aware that things had changed between them, she didn't think it was that serious. Wanting to know why Brian suddenly decided to terminate the marriage, using a private detective and the internet, Nancy uncovered Brian's secret; he had a girlfriend. Although Nancy was hurt and angry, she committed to herself not to let the divorce destroy her. She began a diet and exercise regimen. She began to lose weight. By all accounts she looked great. She felt great.

As the divorce process progressed, things became extremely contentious. Settlement negotiations broke down and reaching an amicable settlement became out of the question. A trial date was set.

In mid-June, Nancy began to experience severe abdominal pain. She finally sought medical intervention. The day before trial commencement, her doctor called her into the office. The diagnosis: stage four cancer which had spread throughout her body. She immediately contacted her lawyer, who was able to revamp the trial presentation contemplating her health condition and prognosis.

Very often, we women put our health and healthcare last. We put the health of everyone else in our lives first. But before you get divorced you must get a handle on what your current health condition is.

## ~~Existing Diagnosis~~

Be clear on your existing known conditions. Make a listing of all existing conditions. Be mindful that some conditions are easily overlooked. This is often the case when a diagnosis was made years prior. Conditions which do not require regular treatment such as ophthalmologic, dental, podiatric, and audiologist conditions are often disregarded. Do not forget to list conditions which require long term care regimens such as asthma, arthritis, or high blood pressure.

## ~~Current Treatment~~

Next ascertain current treatments and medications prescribed. Make inquiry as to prognosis and find out if the condition is degenerative. Has a diet or exercise program been prescribed? If so, is the program being followed? Get as much information as possible.

## ~~Pre-divorce Physical~~

Without exception, I always advise women I work with to get a complete medical examination at the outset of the divorce process. Many find the advice odd, but I firmly believe it is the first and most important pre-divorce step. Many feel that they do not need such a physical because they have not been intimate with their spouse in a while or they believe that their spouse has been faithful. They mistakenly believe that the singular purpose for the physical is to detect the presence of sexually transmitted diseases. The reasons for getting the physical go far beyond STD testing.

First, and foremost, you need to be as healthy as possible. You are going to be under a great deal of stress and you need to be at your best.

Secondly, underlying conditions may surface and hamper your ability to work or support yourself. You must be sure that they are taken into account when determining your future needs.

Thirdly, your insurance coverage may change post-divorce, particularly if the coverage is provided through your soon to be ex-husband's employment. Get necessary medical needs addressed while you still have the coverage in place.

Your medical condition can greatly affect the outcome of your life post divorce.

During the examination, tell the physician that you are contemplating or involved in the divorce process. Be clear that you want a full work up to determine your current medical condition as well as, to the greatest extent possible, your future medical outlook.

### ~~Medical Expenses~~

At this juncture it is wise to get an understanding of your current medical insurance coverage. If you are currently covered by a policy which is available through your husband's employment, understand that once the divorce is final you will not be legally eligible to receive benefits under the policy. If you are in this position, now is the time to begin the process of obtaining coverage. Begin by speaking with your insurance agent to ascertain your options and obtain premium quotes. Pre-existing medical conditions may hamper your ability to obtain coverage. The projected premium cost should be included in your expense calculations.

Many costs associated with healthcare such as nutritional supplements, non-prescription medications, and some medical equipment and supplies are not covered by insurance. Be sure to include these costs in your budget numbers. If you are receiving alternative care such as naturopathic or chiropractic, the costs may not be fully covered by insurance. Be sure to include those costs in your budget. Include co-pays and any other out of pocket medical expenses in your monthly budget.

# Chapter 8

## The Children

*Max and Samantha were both very involved in the raising of their children, 17-year old Travis and 13-year old Brianna. The day to day menagerie of child rearing duties - supervising homework, carpool, and chauffeuring the children to and from their countless activities - were handled by Samantha. Weekends were for family: skiing, movie nights, and barbeques. For years Max was head coach of his son's Pop Warner football team. The children adored their father, and enjoyed spending time with him. This was not the case between Max and Samantha. Over time the relationship between Max and Samantha began to lose its spark. They did not enjoy each other's company beyond family activities. They rarely spent time together. They were living very separate lives. Samantha felt that Max was unsupportive and emotionally unavailable.*

Irrespective of the child's age, parental divorce is by far one of the most difficult and stressful events that can occur during a child's life. Sadly, many moms become consumed by their own feelings, get caught up in the legal process, and fail to deal with the feelings and needs of their children. It is during this most stressful time that you must give the needs of your children priority.

Issues involving custody and parenting are among the most contentious and emotionally charged issues in divorce. Divorce does divide the family unit, but it need not destroy the family.

Separate out your feelings about your husband from your feelings about your children's father. You may believe he is lousy husband, but is he also a lousy father? If he is a good dad, do your children deserve to maintain that relationship?

## ~~Breaking the News to Your Children~~

For your children, divorce takes on a very different meaning than it does for you or your spouse. For you it is the loss of a spouse. For the children it is the loss of the family unit. This can be very disconcerting. It is up to both of you, as parents, to allay their fears and ease the stress.

Give careful consideration to how you will tell the children about the divorce. What is best will depend largely on the children's ages. Ideally, if possible, you and your spouse should tell them jointly. Most importantly, be sure that children understand that your divorce is not their fault. Regardless of age, children always believe that if they had done something differently, the divorce would not happen. Even if you believe they know this is not true, tell them anyway.

## Some Do's and Don'ts to Consider When Breaking the News to your Children:

### Do

- Speak as calmly as possible.
- Reassure them that they are not to blame for the divorce.
- Reassure them of your continued love and affection for them.
- Acknowledge their feelings.
- Allow them to grieve the loss of the family unit.
- Answer their questions.
- Address their concerns.
- Limit the details given regarding the reasons for and the process of the divorce.
- Remember that your child loves both of you.

### Don't

- Speak negatively of the other parent.
- Use your child as your sounding board.
- Attempt to gain your child's allegiance.
- Overburden them with the minutia of the process.
- Discuss the details of the reasons for the divorce.
- Make your child choose a side.

## ~~Co-Parenting Through the Divorce Process~~

Although the marital relationship between you and your spouse will come to a screeching halt, the relationship between your children and their father will, and should, continue. Undeniably and understandably, continuing to co-parent with your soon to be ex-husband can be very challenging. Unless the physical or emotional safety of your child would truly be compromised by continued contact, you must not hamper the continued relationship.

First, figure out what the current parenting practices are. What is the pick up and drop off school routine? Who generally attends school meetings and other appointments? Will there be ways for these norms to continue during the divorce process and once it is final? If your current parenting practices are working well, why change them dramatically?

## 10 Tips for Effective Co-Parenting During the Divorce Process

- Do not discuss the specifics of the divorce process with your children.
- Do not use your children as a shoulder to cry on.
- Do not use your children as bargaining chips.
- Do not use your children as messengers.
- Continue to be a good parent.
- Try to be as cooperative and flexible as possible.
- Try to keep transitions to a minimum.
- Do not use your children as spies.
- Do not quiz your children about their father.
- Allow your children to enjoy time spent with their father.

### ~~Special Needs Children~~

Often there are additional costs associated with meeting the needs of special needs children. These costs may include educational advocates, therapeutic programs, tutors, and therapists. Be sure to include such costs when ascertaining expenses. Many of these expenses can be very high and are often unreimbursed.

### ~~College Students~~

If you have a child currently enrolled in college or other post-secondary education, remember to consider the payment of tuition and fees in calculating your current expenses. In the event that you and your spouse have co-signed for a student loan or taken out a parent loan, include those loans in ascertaining your liabilities. Include such loans in the liability calculation even if repayment is deferred.

# *Chapter 9*

## *Other Considerations*

### ~~Insurance Coverage During Divorce~~

Ongoing insurance coverage is often overlooked during divorce. You must be vigilant in maintaining adequate coverage. Start by inventorying all of the insurance coverage you and your husband now carry: auto, health, life, long term care and disability. It is important to understand the policy limitations as well as terms and conditions of coverage.

It is not uncommon for spouses to wrongly cease payment of insurance premiums during the divorce process. Do not rely solely on your husband's word that payments are being made. Protect yourself; get copies of all payment receipts. Always double check with the carrier to ensure coverage is in place. It is advisable to check each time a premium is due. Once a policy is canceled due to non payment, if reinstatement is possible, it will likely be costly to do so.

## ~~Insurance Coverage Post Divorce~~

Determine which insurances will need to be replaced or altered post divorce. Meet with your insurance agent as early in the process as possible to develop a post divorce insurance plan which will address your needs. Consider auto, life, health, disability and long term care insurances.

In the event you anticipate receiving alimony or child support, obtaining life and disability insurance to secure payments in the event of your husband's death or disability is a must.

If your employer offers health, disability or life insurance, inquire early on in the process about any necessary coverage and premium changes.

## ~~Business Owners~~

**Joint Business Owners:** Owning a business with your spouse can be a mixed blessing. When things are going well, having time flexibility and working as a team can be wonderful benefits. However, during divorce being business partners can add a challenging dimension.

During the divorce it is often necessary to keep business operations going. This is extremely tough; while part of your life is falling apart, you must keep another part up and running as normal. Just as it is unwise to mix business and pleasure, it is unwise to mix business and displeasure. The number one rule for continuing business operation during divorce: keep personal issues out of business.

**Some Do's and Don'ts to Consider For Working Together During the Divorce Process:**

**Do**

- Keep the business relationship professional.
- Respect your husband as a business partner.
- Maintain a positive working environment.
- Continue to provide optimal service.
- Continue to produce optimal products.

**Don'ts**

- Discuss personal issues with your spouse at work.
- Burden employees or co-workers with details of your divorce.
- Attempt to turn employees and co-workers into your allies.
- Speak disparagingly about your husband.
- Compromise the goodwill or integrity of the business.

At this juncture it is important to speak with your business accountant and attorney to determine the condition of the business.

**Five questions to ask the accountant:**

1. What is the current fiscal health of the business? Review the last three years of tax returns as well as a current profit and loss statement (P&L).

2. What are the tax considerations associated with continued joint ownership, sale or buyout?

3. What is the current debt?

4. Is there any personal liability?

5. What is the value of the business?

**Five questions to ask the lawyer:**

1. What is the actual legal structure of the business?

2. What is the actual ownership interest division?

3. Are there any expected suits to be filed?

4. Are there any outstanding judgments?

5. Is there any personal liability?

**If You Own a Business or Are in a Partnership:** If you are a business owner, your priority must be protecting the business. Hopefully, business and personal assets have not been commingled to a point of being considered marital assets (i.e., used significant marital funds to launch or float the business). As part of your preparation for divorce meet with your business attorney and accountant to determine exactly where you stand financially and legally.

Be sure to speak to your business partners as soon into the process as possible. Ideally the partnership agreement will address the protocol in the event of a partner's divorce. If the agreement is silent on the issue, it is imperative to immediately establish an operational protocol.

**Five questions to ask the accountant:**

1. What is the current fiscal health of the business? Review the last 3 years tax returns as well as a current profit and loss statement (P&L).

2. What are the tax considerations of continued operation, sale, or buyout?

3.  What is the current debt?

4.  Is there any personal debt liability?

5.  What is the value of the business?

**Six questions to ask the lawyer:**

1.  What is the actual legal structure of the business?

2.  What is the actual ownership interest division?

3.  Are there any expected suits to be filed?

4.  Are there any outstanding judgments

5.  Is there any personal liability?

6.  Is any part of the business or practice considered to be a marital asset?

**If Your Spouse Owns a Business or is in Partnership:** As soon as possible you must determine your rights as well as your liability, if any. It is wise to consult with an accountant, business valuator or attorney to independently advise you where you are.

**Eleven questions to ask your team members:**

1.  What is the current fiscal health of the business? Review the last 3 years tax returns as well as a current profit and loss statement (P&L).

2.  Is there any personal debt liability?

3.  What is the actual legal structure of the business?

4.  What is the actual ownership interest?

5.  Is there any personal liability?

6.  Is any part of the business be considered to be a marital asset?

7. What is the value of your husband's interest?

8. Has there been any recent changes in ownership?

9. Have there been any recent changes in your spouse's income received from the business?

10. Has your spouse loaned the business any money?

11. Has your spouse made any additional capital contributions?

## ~~Uncovering Hidden Business Assets and Income~~

If you have any reason to know of or suspect that your husband has hidden business assets or income, take every possible measure to uncover them. Review past business records and filings with your accountant and attorney to ascertain if there has been an unexplainable decrease in business revenue. Look at bank records to uncover transactions which may be improper or inconsistent with ordinary business practices.

If you do not have access to records and filings, have your attorney subpoena them. Do not allow time to alter or destroy records. Have the subpoenas served as soon as possible. If necessary, have your attorney file motions with the court to obtain an order protecting the records from being destroyed or altered.

Consider hiring a forensic accountant to locate any hidden assets. Forensic accounting, also known as investigative accounting, focuses not only on the reported books and records but also on evidence of fraudulent or improper accounting practices.

**Step Two Summary**

Step two of *What Now? Divorce Planning* is by far the most laborious of all the steps due to necessary massive data and information collection and analysis.

> **The goals of step two which should have been achieved are:**
>
> 1. Clarify current financial status and needs.
>
> 2. Ascertained your current legal standing and identified any legal issues.
>
> 3. Ascertained your current health state.
>
> 4. Begin to assess the best interests of your children.

# STEP THREE

## Your Needs and Wants

# *Chapter 10*

## *Your Future Needs*

Before you start the divorce process you must have a clear understanding of what you want and of what you need. Keep in mind that, in divorce, like many other areas of life, needs are very different than wants. Needs are "must have's", wants are "would like's". Do not confuse the two. Never compromise or bargain away a need to get a want. You may likely regret it when the divorce dust settles.

### 5 Questions to Ask Yourself When Distinguishing Needs from Wants

1. Will my ability to reasonably support myself and (or) my children be negatively affected?

2. Is my physical or emotional well-being jeopardized?

3. Are my legal rights in jeopardy?

4. One year from now, how will I be affected?

5. Will this affect my long term financial goals?

The next step is to figure out what you need. Get clear on what your immediate survival must have's are as well as your long term survival must have's. Included in your list of needs should be day to day financial survival, insurance, and payment of debt.

## Must Have's Include:

- Day to day financial survival.
- Payment of debt.
- Life insurance.
- Medical insurance.
- Retirement planning.
- Payment of taxes.
- Plan in the event of premature death or disability of your spouse.

## ~~Day to Day Financial Survival~~

Ascertaining day to day financial needs requires significant futuristic planning. While it may be impossible to precisely calculate your post divorce financial needs, make every effort to determine your needs as closely as possible. Included in day to day financial needs should be housing, utilities, food, personal hygiene and transportation.

**Housing:** First, determine if you will remain in the marital home. This decision must be a financial decision and not an emotional decision. In short, ask yourself if you can afford the rent or mortgage and the associated costs? If not, immediately start looking for suitable housing which you can afford. When ascertaining the cost of shelter, be sure to include property taxes, homeowner's or renter's insurance, maintenance and upkeep.

**Utilities:** In order to project future costs, ascertain the cost of the prior year's utility payments. Once you have ascertained this amount, add 10-20% to account for rate hikes. A common mistake made in projecting post divorce cost is to divide the cost paid in half. In actuality it is unlikely that your utility usage will be cut in half; therefore, the cost will not be cut in half. For example, heating cost is based on the cost of heating a dwelling and not the number of people in the home.

**Food:** Determine the average monthly expenditure over the last 12-month period. This figure is a good starting base. Similar to utilities, it is unwise to divide the total household cost in half. Do not forget to include the cost of eating out or your daily coffee run.

**Transportation:** Include gas, oil, upkeep and loan or lease payments.

### ~~Payment of Debt and Taxes~~

In most states, married couples are able to incur debt jointly as well as individually. It is imperative to provide for the payment of debt in your *What Now? Strategic Divorce Plan*. Begin by ascertaining the debts for which you have personal liability. This will include debts which are owned by you and your spouse as well as any debt in which you are solely responsible. Review your credit report to be sure you are taking all debt into account.

The payment of taxes must be considered. Included should be property tax and personal income tax. Be aware that alimony is considered taxable income to the recipient. Account for this tax liability in your calculations.

## ~~Insurance Coverage~~

**Life Insurance:** To protect your children in the event of your premature death, you must have an adequate amount of life insurance coverage in place. Speak to your insurance agent as soon as possible to ascertain the amount of coverage needed. Be sure to include the premium amount in your monthly budget.

**Medical Insurance:** Maintaining medical insurance for you and your children is a must. If you are currently covered by a policy provided through your husband's employer, you will need to obtain your own medical insurance. If you are unable to secure insurance through your employer, you will need to obtain private insurance which may be very costly. Speak to an agent to determine the cost of the coverage. Include the cost in your calculations of future needs.

**Auto Insurance:** Throughout your marriage you have probably been covered under a joint policy with your husband. Once the divorce is final, you will need to obtain individual coverage. Be sure to speak to your agent to ensure a lapse in coverage does not occur.

## ~~Retirement Planning~~

Often focused exclusively on the present, many women disregard the need to plan for retirement. It is wise to have your financial planner or advisor draw up a projection of retirement needs. Regardless of how old you are at the time of your divorce you need to be prepared for your future.

## ~~Credit Protection and Building~~

Your credit rating will significantly impact your ability to move forward post divorce. Get a handle on your credit situation. Carefully review your credit report. Is all of the information accurate? Now is the time to address any credit issues. Divorce can take a toll on credit ratings. If necessary, put a plan in place to repair your credit.

Many married women have not obtained individual credit; all credit is maintained jointly with their husband. It is strongly recommended that you begin to build your own credit. Apply for a credit card as soon as possible. The sooner you begin to build your own credit history the better.

## ~~Plan in the Event of Premature Death or Disability of Your Spouse~~

In the event of the premature death or disability of your spouse, you will still be in need of child support and/or alimony. Failing to plan for the premature death or disability of a spouse is one of the greatest avoidable mistakes of divorce. None of us has a crystal ball to see into the future; however, we should prepare for as many possible *what if's* as possible. The premature death or disability is a *what if* that is easily planned for. It is imperative that life and disability insurance coverage is in place.

**Life Insurance:** You must have life insurance covering the life of your soon to be ex-husband. The coverage amount should be sufficient to cover alimony and child support in the event of his death during the period of payment. You should be the named irrevocable beneficiary. It is wise to be the owner of the policy. By being the owner of the policy you will be able to ensure that the beneficiary can not be changed without your permission. Also as owner, you will be notified if the policy is canceled due to non payment of premiums. You will maintain control.

**Disability Insurance:** Provides for continued income in the event of inability to work due to an extended illness or disability. Benefits received under the policy generally replace a percentage of income. Be sure that your spouse has ample disability coverage in place. In the event such coverage is not in place, insist on the purchase of a disability policy. It is also advisable to include an emergency savings plan which can be utilized while you wait to receive benefits.

# Chapter 11

## Your "Would Likes"

*Throughout their 23-year marriage, Kathleen and Rob frequently disagreed over Rob's excessive spending on what Kathleen dubbed 'useless toys.' During the marriage, Rob spent thousands of dollars purchasing such things as motorcycles and expensive sporting and technology equipment. Of all of the items, Rob's prized possession was his 26-foot sailboat valued at $27,000.00. Kathleen, who loathed sailing, had only sailed with Rob 3 times. When their divorce negotiations became acrimonious, each of them set on a course of hurting each other and began acting out of spite and greed. Kathleen lost sight of what was truly important to her and became reactionary and retaliatory. Knowing that losing the boat would be devastating to Rob, Kathleen made a demand for the boat. Not wanting to lose the boat, Rob offered Kathleen an additional $30,000.00, in cash, if she would allow him to retain the boat. Kathleen foolishly turned down the offer, and continued to fight for the boat. Unable to reach agreement, the case went to trial. Following three days of testimony and $43,000.00 in attorney fees, the judge ordered that Rob would retain the boat and pay to Kathleen one half of the value of the boat: $13,500.00.*

Often assets are used as yet another weapon in the emotional tug of war of divorce. Often the desire for a certain asset is based upon revenge, inflicting pain, or spite. As was the case for Kathleen, this could prove imprudent. Don't do it.

## ~~Asset Division~~

The division of assets often becomes the "who gets what" war. Couples frequently spend hours negotiating the distribution of assets, and much of this time is unnecessary. It does not make financial or logical sense to spend a thousand dollars in legal fees to negotiate who gets a 20 year old couch that is worth fifty dollars. By the same token, it does not make financial or logical sense to insist on retaining an asset for which you cannot afford the upkeep. If you and your husband are unable to make the monthly mortgage payments together, it is unrealistic to think you will be able to do so on your own. Therefore, keeping the house may not be prudent.

The correct way to figure out which assets you will pursue during negotiations and/or trial is to base the decision on financial and practical logic. For each asset ask yourself five questions:

1.  Do I truly want this item for reasons which are not meant to hurt my spouse?

2.  Does retaining the asset make financial sense?

3.  Does retaining the asset make practical sense?

4.  Does the personal or financial value of the asset outweigh the financial cost of fighting for the item?

5.  Can I afford the cost upkeep of the asset?

## 9 Critical Mistakes to Avoid:

1. Making decisions based on emotion.

2. Not understanding the tax consequences associated with certain assets.

3. Fighting over assets which do not have any real value - personal or financial.

4. Seeking assets solely to hurt your spouse.

5. Seeking assets solely out of revenge or spite.

6. Insisting on retaining assets which you cannot afford to retain.

7. Foregoing a 'must have' in order to obtain a 'would like'.

8. Retaining an asset which does not make financial sense to keep.

9. Retaining assets which do not make logistical sense to keep.

## Real Estate

**The Marital Home:** In most cases the marital residence is the largest asset and is often the most hotly contentious asset to divide. All too frequently, women allow emotional attachment to the house cloud their judgment in determining the best course of action when considering dividing the house.

In divorce there are three ways to effectively divide the marital home:

1. Sell the property and divide the proceeds.

2. One spouse buys out the interest of the other.

3. One spouse remains in the marital home until a date in the future, and then sells the property and divides the proceeds.

Should you choose to remain in the home, be sure that you are able to afford not only the mortgage payment but also all associated cost. The associated cost includes property taxes, homeowner's insurance, landscaping, snow removal, and general upkeep.

If you know you are unable to actually afford the carrying cost of the home, think long and hard before you fight to get the house. Being forced into foreclosure can be disastrous. Do not get in over your head because of an emotional attachment to your house.

**Vacation Homes and Time Shares:** As with your primary residence, think long and hard about the sensibility and feasibility of retaining vacation homes and time shares. While you may have wonderful memories of time spent at a vacation home or time share facility, can you now afford the associated cost on your own?

**Investment or Business Real Estate:** Investment and business real estate is just that, an investment. During the divorce process, it is advisable to continue to treat investment property and business real estate as a business transaction. Determine the value from a business standpoint. Does it make financial and logistical sense to retain the property? Or in the alternative, does selling to a third party or having your spouse buy out your interest make better sense? With investment real estate carefully calculate the carrying cost of management, maintenance, and upkeep. Be sure to consider the personal time commitment required to manage and maintain the property.

## Liquid Assets

Liquid assets are those assets which are in cash form or easily convertible to cash. Included are bank accounts, credit union accounts, stocks and bonds. Some collectibles such as coins and artwork which can be easily sold are also considered liquid assets. Liquid assets are perhaps the easiest of assets to divide. Simply determine the asset percentage split between you and your spouse then apply the percentage to the total.

For example:

Total Liquid Assets $375,000.00

Agreed split: 50-50% division

Each party receives $187, 500.00

## Retirement Plans

Retirement accounts include, but are not limited to, IRA's, Keogh, and profit sharing, pensions and 401(k) and annuity plans. Similar to liquid assets, such accounts are generally divided based upon a percentage split. Many states allow funds accumulated prior to the marriage to be excluded from the divisible pot.

Be mindful that premature withdrawals from retirement accounts often result in tax and other fees and penalties. Be sure to consult with your financial professional team members to determine exposure.

Using the asset inventory completed in step 2 of your *What Now? Tactical Divorce Plan*, take an objective look at the assets and determine which of the assets you truly have an interest in retaining. Develop a prioritized list of personal assets you wish to retain. Be reasonable and practical.

Personal property includes household furnishings, jewelry, motor vehicles, heirlooms, keepsakes, sports and hobby equipment. Because of the emotional component attached to the things we hold dear, dividing personal items is often stressful and extremely discordant. The division is often spite-driven. While you may feel vindicated by retaining your husband's prized possession, is it really worth it? You will be much better served by making decisions based on logic and not vengeance.

## ~~Allocation of Debts and Liabilities~~

Similar to the division of assets, many couples spend countless hours negotiating the allocation of debts and liabilities. Much of this time is unnecessary. Using the delineation of debts and liabilities developed in step 2, work to find a reasonable and fair allocation. Be sure to speak to your financial team member regarding any tax consequences which may be associated with any debts or liabilities.

If you are having difficulty or are unable to pay your debts, it is strongly advised that you seek debt counseling or a bankruptcy attorney.

## ~~Jumpstart for Your Post Divorce Life~~

For many women divorce necessitates the need to work outside of the home. If you have not worked outside of the home for some time, there may be a need to obtain additional education or training. Consider having the cost of such training or education included in your divorce agreement.

If you decide to start a business, consider having the start up cost included in your divorce agreement.

There may be tax benefits to receiving these in exchange for a reduced alimony as they may not be considered taxable income.

## ~~The Children's Expenses~~

Beyond child support, you may want to consider other expenses incurred on behalf of the children. Such costs include, but are certainly not limited to, extra-curricular activities, lessons, summer camps, enrichment programs, clothing, school supplies, school lunches, field trips, purchasing gifts for friends, and auto insurance. Many parents divide these costs equally or proportionally to income.

For example, if Mom's net income is $94,000/year and Dad's net income is $72,000/year, the allocation of payment would be:

Mom: 57%
Dad: 43%

If your children are young, remember to also consider childcare cost.

## ~~Post Majority Education~~

Several states provide for the payment of post majority education for children of divorce; however, most states do not. If your state does not have such a provision, and it is contemplated that your child will pursue post secondary education or training, consider providing for the payment in your divorce agreement. Remember to consider not only the cost of tuition but all associated cost and fees.

# *Chapter 12*

## *Get Clear About Wants and Needs*

*Patricia and Tim, embroiled in a very contentious divorce, were both set on a course to emotionally, legally and financially break the other. They fought bitterly over every issue of the divorce, from the significant: parenting time and retirement account division, to the trivial issues: who would retain the lawnmower and how to divide the pots and pans. It was truly a test of wills and a game of one upmanship. Anything that was seemingly important to one, the other was determined to have. Of real importance to Tim was his DVD collection. Patricia, well aware of this, set out to win the DVD collection. Losing sight of what her actual needs and wants were, she negotiated away her rights to cash assets which she needed in order to begin her new life. She also gave up truly valuable personal items in an effort to obtain the collection. When settlement was reached, Patricia did receive 50% of the collection. Unbeknownst to her, the part of the collection she agreed to take was made up of newer replaceable DVDs. In short, easily replaceable by Tim.*

It is highly unlikely that you will successfully negotiate or be awarded everything you want. You must prioritize and set goals and parameters to ensure the settlement reached meets your basic needs and that some wants are achieved. Because settlement negotiations often occur over time in fragmentary piecemeal fashion, it can be difficult to keep sight of the big picture. When negotiations become complex, which they generally do, having a guidepost will help you to maintain focus and be goal directed. Prioritizing and setting parameters will help you and your team members to understand what will truly work for you.

## ~~Prioritizing Your Needs~~

Utilizing the delineation of needs and wants developed in step three, determine priority ranking for each item. Remember needs always, always, always take significance over wants.

Next, carefully review your needs. For each item ask yourself if it is a real need or something that you could do without. Once you have established a final listing of needs, categorize them into the following categories:

**Day to day financial survival:** Include mortgages, taxes, utilities, food, transportation, property upkeep, and maintenance. Also include any other expenses which are necessary for your basic living and comfort. Such items may include fitness programs, educational expenses, un-reimbursed medical expenses and medications.

**Debt:** Include credit card debt, car loan and lease payments and student loans. Also include any other debt which you are liable to pay. Provisions for the payment of joint marital debt must be included in the final divorce settlement agreement. Do not acquiesce under pressure and sign an agreement that does not have such a provision.

**Insurances:** Include medical, disability, auto, life, and long-term disability for yourself. Also include life and disability insurance covering your spouse in case of his disability or premature death.

**Retirement Savings:** Include 401(k), pension, annuity and SEP accounts. Remember to consider the continued funding of accounts post divorce.

Once you have categorized each item, begin prioritizing within each category. Your personal scenario will dictate the priority order.

Finally, develop a list of absolute non-negotiable items. These are the things that you must have and cannot be flexible with. When developing this list reasonableness is a must. While food is a necessity, dining at 5-star restaurants is not. Do not confuse crucial needs with potential needs. While there may be an immediate need to repair a leaky roof, there may only be a potential need to replace the roof. Also cosmetic repairs are generally not crucial.

### ~~Prioritizing Your Wants~~

**Liquid Assets and Retirement Accounts:** When prioritizing which liquid assets you want, carefully consider tax and other ramifications of receiving the assets. The objective is to seek liquid assets which can be utilized in the present and/or have a future value.

**Personal Items and Household Items:** Because there is often an emotional component attached to personal items, they are often difficult to prioritize. When contemplating which personal items you want, do a cost benefit analysis. Does retaining the item justify the cost of getting and retaining it? Costs to consider include legal fees, upkeep and maintenance. Also consider the logic of retaining an item. Fighting for the riding mower when you will be moving into a condominium does not make sense. It is not uncommon for some couples to get caught up the division of what many lawyers term 'pots and pans', and spend thousands of dollars in legal fees to win them. It is imprudent to argue over replaceable items or those which do not have a value that justify the cost. The true exception to this rule is family heirlooms, and other irreplaceable significant items.

Once you have completed a cost benefit analysis of personal and household items, develop a priority rank list.

Once you have completed your priority list, look over it to determine if there are any nonnegotiable items. Again, be reasonable. Make a nonnegotiable list.

## ~~Setting Goals~~

Setting goals is very important. It is advisable to develop three settlement position statements: ideal, likely, and bare minimum of acceptable. These statements are not meant to share with your soon to be ex-husband. It is never wise to show all of your cards. These lists are strictly to give you and your team members clarity and parameters for negotiating.

## Statement One: The Ultimate

Include:

- Nonnegotiable needs.
- Nonnegotiable wants.
- The high of your negotiable needs (add 25-35% to your actual needs)
- The high of your negotiable wants.

## Statement Two: The Likely

Include:

- Nonnegotiable needs.
- Nonnegotiable wants.
- Actual needs.
- The top 50% of wanted items on your priority list.

## Statement Three: Bare Minimum

Include:

- Nonnegotiable needs.
- Nonnegotiable wants.
- The bare minimum of needs (reduce needs as practical, 10-15%).
- The top 25% of wants.

# *Chapter 13* ■

## *Custody and Parenting*

Deciding child custody and parental access are often among the most contentious and emotionally charged aspects of divorce. As mothers, we instinctively seek to protect our children from any harm. It has often been said that hell hath no fury like a women scorned, not true, hell hath no fury like a mother who believes her child is in danger or in pain. I truly believe most mothers would fight a grizzly bear to protect their child. Many women believe that the person they are divorcing has not only treated them badly, but has also mistreated their children. Often this is used as justification to limit the father's involvement in the lives of the children. You must put the needs of your children first. Is the best interest of your children served by limiting involvement with their father? In most cases, it is not.

Understandably it is often difficult to separate out your feelings toward your husband from your feelings toward your children's father; however, to ensure that the best interest of your children is served you must. It is wise to take an objective historical view. Jar your memory for better times by looking back at family photos. Are your children happy and content spending time with their father? Many divorce mediators and judges require parents to view photos of their children while negotiating custodial and access arrangements, so as to remain mindful of the children's needs. This may be a place for someone in your personal support team to lend some help. Hopefully, they will be able to look at the situation with greater objectivity and talk you through it.

### ~~Custody~~

When contemplating the form of custody which will work best for your family, first ascertain the forms of custodial arrangements utilized in your state. Many states continue to promote custody arrangements which award physical custody to one parent and allow the other parent visitation rights. Some states have moved toward shared custody arrangements. Shared parenting arrangements allow for parents to have equal or near equal time with the children.

Once you have ascertained the available forms of custody in your state, determine the form which will best serve the needs of your family.

The type of custody which is appropriate for your family is the form that ensures that the best interest of your children will be served. As the parent, you must promote the wellbeing of your children.

Some things to consider when ascertaining the best interest of your children include:

1. Ages of the children.
2. Genders of the children.
3. Emotional state and needs of the children.
4. The parent-child relationship.
5. Special needs of the children.

Remember divorce should restructure the family unit; it should not destroy it.

In broad terms three forms of child custody exist:

**Sole custody:** One parent has exclusive custodial rights and responsibilities. This includes, but is not limited to, making day to day parenting decisions as well as major decisions regarding health, education and welfare. Unless proven to be a danger to the child, the non-custodial parent is granted visitation time with the children. This type of custody is often utilized in cases of parental inability to communicate, or when the physical and or emotional safety of the children is at risk.

**Joint legal custody:** the most common form of custody. Children live with one parent. Parents have equal say in the making of major decisions. Both parents have access to medical, school and other official records. It is crucial that parents are able to effectively communicate regarding the children's health, education and welfare. This is not to say parents must agree all of the time, just that they are able to communicate directly with each other or with the assistance of a third party. Almost without exception, both parents are granted physical time with the children.

**Joint legal and physical custody:** Also referred to as shared custody, joint legal and physical custody allows both parents to remain very involved in the day to day aspects of child rearing. Parents with shared custody have equal say in the making of major decisions as well as day to day decisions. In addition, shared parenting allows parents to have equal or near equal physical time with the children. Children who participate in shared parenting arrangements generally travel between the parents' homes for predetermined blocks of time. It is imperative that parents are able to communicate effectively. It is also necessary for parents to be able to co-parent regarding day to day issues.

There are many upsides to utilizing this type of custody, such as maximizing the time spent with each parent, and allowing both parents to actively participate in day to day child rearing responsibilities. However, there are some downsides that should be considered. Because the children will move from home to home, there will be a need for duplicity of basic items. Purchasing two sets of clothes, toys, and other necessities can prove to be costly. In addition, frequent transitions (such as going from house to house) may be difficult for some children.

## 5 Key Things to Remember When Contemplating Custody:

1. Your children love both you and your husband.

2. In most cases children benefit from maintaining a strong relationship with both parents.

3. Deciding on custody arrangements out of spite or revenge is wrong.

4. Your children should not be used as weapons.

5. Parental divorce should not result in the loss of relationship with either parent.

## ~~Parenting~~

Continuing to co-parent with your ex-husband can be very challenging. For the sake of your children's wellbeing, you must put aside your differences and find a way to work cooperatively and peaceably. Albeit this is often easier said than done, you must make the needs of your children a priority.

### Some areas to consider are:

- How are pick-up and drop-offs handled?
- What interactions will each parent have with the child's school?
- Are there any sports or activities that the child shall not be allowed to participate in?
- The involvement of new significant others in the life of the children.
- How will day to day educational, religious and social decisions be made?
- How will major educational, medical and religious decisions be made?

## ~~Parental Access Plans~~

Parental access plans, often referred to as visitation plans, set forth the time to be spent with the children by each parent. There are as many parental access plans as there are families; your family plan should be tailored to meet the needs of your family.

Some factors to consider when crafting the parental access plan may include:

1. Proximity of parents' homes.
2. Work hours of parents.
3. Academic and social needs of the children.
4. Personal needs of the parents.
5. Parenting strengths and weaknesses.

Some common parental access plans include:

- The children reside with one parent and spend time with the other parent on weekends, often sharing mid-week dinner(s).
- The children alternate weeks living with each parent.
- The children live with each parent 3.5 days each week.
- Bird nesting: the children live in the marital home and each parent 'flies in' to spend time with the children.

It is unwise to develop a plan which allows for an equal division of time between parents solely to promote parental fairness. Allow consistency and normalcy. Think back when you were at the age of your child - what would have worked for you? You must allow your child a childhood which is not consumed by divorce and its issues.

Here are some sample parenting plans.

## Alternate Weeks

| | Mon | Tues | Wed | Thurs | Fri | Sat | Sun |
|---|---|---|---|---|---|---|---|
| Week 1 Mom | Mon (Mom) | Tues (Mom) | Wed (Mom) | Thurs (Mom) | Fri (Mom) | Sat (Mom) | Sun (Mom) |
| Week 2 Dad | Mon (Dad) | Tues (Dad) | Wed (Dad) | Thurs (Dad) | Fri (Dad) | Sat (Dad) | Sun (Dad) |
| Week 3 Mom | Mon (Mom) | Tues (Mom) | Wed (Mom) | Thurs (Mom) | Fri (Mom) | Sat (Mom) | Sun (Mom) |
| Week 4 Dad | Mon (Dad) | Tues (Dad) | Wed (Dad) | Thurs (Dad) | Fri (Dad) | Sat (Dad) | Sun (Dad) |

## Mid-week Transition

| | Mon | Tues | Wed | Thurs | Fri | Sat | Sun |
|---|---|---|---|---|---|---|---|
| Week 1 | Mon (Mom) | Tues (Mom) | Wed (Mom/Dad) | Thurs (Dad) | Fri (Dad) | Sat (Dad) | Sun (Mom) |
| Week 2 | Mon (Mom) | Tues (Mom) | Wed (Mom/Dad) | Thurs (Dad) | Fri (Dad) | Sat (Dad) | Sun (Mom) |
| Week 3 | Mon (Mom) | Tues (Mom) | Wed (Mom/Dad) | Thurs (Dad) | Fri (Dad) | Sat (Dad) | Sun (Mom) |
| Week 4 | Mon (Mom) | Tues (Mom) | Wed (Mom/Dad) | Thurs (Dad) | Fri (Dad) | Sat (Dad) | Sun (Mom) |

## Mid-week Transition/Alternate Weekends

| | Mon | Tues | Wed | Thurs | Fri | Sat | Sun |
|---|---|---|---|---|---|---|---|
| Week 1 | Mon (Mom) | Tues (Mom) | Wed (Dad) | Thurs (Dad) | Fri (Mom) | Sat (Mom) | Sun (Mom) |
| Week 2 | Mon (Mom) | Tues (Mom) | Wed (Dad) | Thurs (Dad) | Fri (Dad) | Sat (Dad) | Sun (Dad) |
| Week 3 | Mon (Mom) | Tues (Mom) | Wed (Dad) | Thurs (Dad) | Fri (Mom) | Sat (Mom) | Sun (Mom) |
| Week 4 | Mon (Mom) | Tues (Mom) | Wed (Dad) | Thurs (Dad) | Fri (Dad) | Sat (Dad) | Sun (Dad) |

## Traditional

| | Mon | Tues | Wed | Thurs | Fri | Sat | Sun |
|---|---|---|---|---|---|---|---|
| Week 1 | Mon (Custodial Parent) | Tues (Custodial Parent) | Wed (Custodial Parent) | Thurs (Custodial Parent) | Fri (Mom) | Sat (Mom) | Sun (Mom) |
| Week 2 | Mon (Custodial Parent) | Tues (Custodial Parent) | Wed (Custodial Parent) | Thurs (Custodial Parent) | Fri (Dad) | Sat (Dad) | Sun (Dad) |
| Week 3 | Mon (Custodial Parent) | Tues (Custodial Parent) | Wed (Custodial Parent) | Thurs (Custodial Parent) | Fri (Mom) | Sat (Mom) | Sun (Mom) |
| Week 4 | Mon (Custodial Parent) | Tues (Custodial Parent) | Wed (Custodial Parent) | Thurs (Custodial Parent) | Fri (Dad) | Sat (Dad) | Sun (Dad) |

## Step Three Summary

Step three has required a great deal of futuristic contemplation and planning. While this may have seemed nebulous at times, this proactive forward thinking and planning has put you in a position to move toward specific goals and objectives. You are now keenly aware of what you need and what you want.

### The goals of step three which should have been achieved are:

1. Ascertain your needs for future survival.
2. Identify your wants.
3. Prioritize your needs and wants.
4. Contemplate continued parenting of your children post divorce.

# STEP FOUR

## Putting Your Plan Into Action

# Chapter 14

## Working With Your Professional Team

*Two weeks after being served with divorce papers by her husband Tim, Kimberly hired a divorce lawyer to represent her in the divorce. Tim and Kimberly were able to agree on most of the settlement terms. Pursuant to the terms of the settlement agreement, Kimberly would remain in the marital home and assume responsibility for the payment of mortgages, taxes and insurance. Tim would pay her $1,750.00 per week alimony . The retirement accounts and liquid assets were  divided 40% to Tim 60% to Kimberly. Kimberly's plan was to withdraw her portion of the retirement account and utilize the funds to pay- off debt to reduce her monthly expenses. Based upon the advice of her attorney, Kimberly believed the agreement was fair and equitable based upon the totality of circumstance. She gladly signed off on the agreement. The divorce proceeded to finalization very amicably. As it turned out, from a legal standpoint the agreement was workable. However, from a financial standpoint, the settlement could have been much more sensible. The withdrawal of funds from the retirement account carried significant tax consequences, as did the alimony payments received. Much of the retirement funds were eaten by the payment of taxes and early withdrawal penalties. If Kimberly had hired an accountant or financial advisor she would have understood  the financial ramifications of the settlement.*

Like Kimberly, many women assume that their lawyer will address all of the surrounding issues of their divorce and fail to hire additional team members such as an accountant, financial advisor and insurance agent. Because the actual divorce is a legal process, your attorney must be the lead player - not the only player. Lawyers practice law; they are trained and responsible for protecting your legal rights. While there are exceptions, most attorneys are not expertly qualified in accounting, insurance, financial advising or mental health. In the event your case has complexities beyond legal issues, which most cases do, it is strongly advised that you retain the services of an expert in each applicable field. Hopefully, you have expended the time and effort to put together a complete team of professionals. As discussed in chapter four, it is crucial to have team members who can address all of the aspects of your divorce: legal financial, emotional, asset division and the like. If you have not done so, get it done as soon as possible. Do not wait until the end of the process to bring experts on board; their insight and expertise will be helpful throughout the process.

## ~~Getting Your Team to Work as a Team~~

Utilizing a team approach is still not commonplace in the divorce world. For many professionals this may be the first go at it. Some may find it difficult to work as part of a team.

It is recommended that you advise team members that you have retained the services of other professionals and expect that their input and expertise should be sought. A simple e-mail or letter introducing the professionals to one another is a great way to get this team approach started.

The professional ethics rules of most fields require the professional to maintain client information in the strictest of confidence. Fear of violating these ethical canons is a justifiable concern of professionals when asked to work as a member of a team. Many professionals will require written authorization to disclose privileged confidential information. Should you wish certain information to remain confidential, be sure to advise the professional of your desire. Because of the volume of information received by professionals, it is often helpful to put such information in writing. Keep a log of all documents that you provide to each member of your team.

If possible, have at least one joint meeting prior to entering into settlement negotiations. This will ensure that everyone is on the same page and understands the implications of decisions.

## 4 Tips for Getting Team Members to Work as a Team

- Be clear on the role and responsibility of each member.
- Introduce members of the team early in the process.
- Don't pit professionals against each.
- Facilitate communication between team members.

## ~~Conveying Goals to Your Team~~

In order for your team to attain your goals, everyone must have a clear understanding of what your goals and parameters are. Many professionals, particularly very experienced professionals, tend to approach cases in a one size fits all fashion. Given your personal situation, your goals and needs may not fit neatly into the mold. Be very clear as to what you need. It is often very helpful for your professional team to understand your underlying rationale for your goals.

Sharing your completed *What Now? Tactical Divorce Plan* with your team members is a great way to share your goals with them. Make copies for team members so they will have a point of reference on file.

Once you have conveyed your goals, your professionals will advise you as to probability and reasonableness of goals given your specific case fact, local custom and law. Often, people have a tendency to apply the outcome of someone else's divorce and believe their outcome should be a mirror image. They question their professional's knowledge and expertise when they are told a certain goal is unreasonable or unwarranted in their case. Remember your CPA is probably much more adept at handling tax issues than your mother's cousin's best friend who was the bookkeeper at the local dry cleaners. Your attorney is much more familiar with local law and custom than your friend who practices law in another state.

### ~~Keeping Professional Fees Reasonable~~

Many attorneys, accountants and financial advisors charge for services based upon an hourly rate. Billable hours can add up very quickly, but you have the power to keep them in line. Often clients will call or e-mail with issues which do not pertain to the expert's field, for example, calling your attorney for tax help or calling your accountant regarding the legal ramifications of selling an asset. Keep a log of all telephone calls, emails, meetings, court times and all other interactions that require any type of attention or interaction from the members of your professional team. Compare your log with the billing statements you receive to ensure the accuracy of your bill.

## 11 Ways to Keep Fees Down

1. Be prepared for every meeting, conference and court hearing.

2. Provide information and documentation in a timely manner; do not force the professional to chase you to get information and documentation. They will bill you the time it takes to write or call.

3. Make a list of questions prior to making telephone calls or meetings to be sure things are covered.

4. Keep phone calls and emails to a minimum. Only contact when necessary.

5. Try to resolve issues with your spouse when possible. Do not use your professional as a referee to decide day-to-day issues.

6. Get a periodic billing statement to keep track of hours billed.

7. Don't confuse the roles of your professionals.

8. Don't attempt to turn your professional relationship into a personal relationship. If you do strike up a friendship, keep it at a distance until your divorce is complete.

9. Be reasonable and flexible in your settlement demands.

10. Be on time for court and other meetings. Often the billing clock starts ticking at the scheduled time, not when you arrive.

11. Inquire about legwork you may be able to do. Making copies yourself may save billable time and copy fees.

## ~~Dissatisfaction with a Team Member~~

Your team members work for you. If you are dissatisfied with a team member, it is acceptable to make them aware of your dissatisfaction. Do not be concerned with offending a team member. This is your life and you must protect yourself. Start by discussing your areas of concern. Perhaps the concerns can be resolved by having this discussion with the team member.

If your concerns are not resolved to your satisfaction, it is acceptable to terminate professional services. Should you decide to terminate services the following steps may be useful:

1. Put the termination in writing.
2. Retrieve your file from the professional.
3. Advise the remaining team members of the termination.
4. If you are terminating the services of your attorney, and not immediately retaining replacement counsel, it may also be necessary to advise your husband's attorney as well as the court.

# *Chapter 15*

## *Getting Help From Your Personal Support Network*

Undoubtedly, during your divorce process you will experience a myriad of emotions and feelings: fear, shame, embarrassment, sadness. Your emotional pendulum may swing hourly, daily or weekly, swinging from sadness, to relief, to anger, to fear. It is also likely that the legal and financial practicalities of the process will leave you confused and frazzled. These are the times when you will benefit from turning to your personal support people - your inner circle. These people will help you get through the highs and lows as well as process through the practicalities.

### ~~Knowing When to Ask for Support~~

As things heat up, there will be times when you are feel overwhelmed and overburdened as you try to acclimate into your new life and roles: single woman, single mother, full time worker. There will also be times when you feel clueless when it comes to decision making. There will be times when you need to backburner your troubles, to kick back and have a good time. Having a support network in place is crucial, but they will be useless if you don't let them support you. Many people, close friends included, may be reluctant to reach out to someone who is experiencing a life altering situation. The people closest to you may well have the desire to help, but knowing how they can be of help is often elusive. That is where you come in. Let them know how they can help. Remember it is fine to ask for support when you need it. Going it alone will only increase your stress. Your inner circle wants to be there for you. Let them!

### ~~How Your Support Network Can Help~~

From being your sounding board for decision making to listening to you when you just need to vent, there are countless ways your personal support network can help and support you. Some ways your network may be able to help may include:

**Attending court hearings and conferences:** Seeing a friendly face in the back of the courtroom will make you feel much more comfortable. If decisions are to be made at the hearing, having someone you trust to bounce ideas off is often helpful.

**Helping out with your children:** Having an extra set of hands to shuttle your children to and from school, extracurricular activities or taking on an extra carpool turn can be quite a relief. Preparing a meal, running errands - sometimes even the most mundane simple tasks can be arduous. Having someone else complete them for you can go a long way in reducing the burden.

**Attending meetings:** the sheer volume and complexity of information received during a conference with your lawyer, financial advisor, or accountant can be dauntingly overwhelming.

Having a second set of ears and eyes to help you process and understand the information during and after the meeting is beneficial.

**Sharing downtime:** Taking time away from thoughts and happenings of your divorce, for a day or just a couple of hours, is often what is needed to gain clarity and focus. Having lunch, grabbing a cup of coffee or catching a movie with a friend are great ways to take your mind off things.

**Listening to you:** Sometimes we need to share our thoughts and feelings. Being there to listen while you cry it out, shout it out or talk it out is a wonderful way for your friends to help you.

**Some Do's and Don'ts to consider when working with your personal support network are:**

**Do's**

- Ask for help when you need it.

- Be open to receiving support.

- Let your friends support you.

- Be specific about what your needs are.

- Remind your friends of how much you value and appreciate their support.

- Remember, once information is disseminated you can't take it back. Be mindful of what information you share.

## Don'ts

- Overburden your friends.
- Bore them with every detail.
- Let your divorce be the sole focus of the relationship.
- Become angry should they not agree with every action or decision.
- Keep negative people in your inner circle.
- Be demanding of their time.

# *Chapter 16*

## *Reaching an Amicable Settlement*

The benefits of reaching an amicable settlement always outweigh the financial and emotional toll of having the terms of your divorce decided by a judge after a drawn out trial. Remember you and your husband, better than anyone, including the judge, know what is best for your family. In reality your divorce is just another case to the lawyers and judges. They will move on to the next matter. For you and your family the end results will have long term impact.

The benefits of reaching settlement are numerous and include:

**Lower cost:** The cost of legal fees and other professional fees associated with trying your case can be astronomical and financially devastating.

**Greater control:** You and your spouse maintain control over how the rest of your life will play out.

**Greater privacy:** In the majority of states court proceedings are open for public viewing. By reaching a settlement you will maintain greater privacy.

**Reduced emotional stress:** Giving and hearing hours of testimony, detailing each and every personal, intimate detail of your marriage can be very grueling and emotionally stressful.

In all cases, reaching a mutually acceptable workable settlement rests on the reasonableness and willingness of both spouses.

## ~~Getting Through Negotiations~~

During your divorce process, every effort should be made to reach an amicable settlement. Generally, your lawyer will engage in negotiations with your soon to be ex-husband's attorney in an effort to settle all of the issues of your divorce, including financial arrangements, division of assets and liabilities, child custody and parenting. The negotiations occur through a series of letters, e-mails and telephone conversations between the lawyers.

Your attorney is duty bound to keep you abreast of the progress. It may also be useful to have your attorney copy you on all written communications with opposing counsel. File these communications in an organized fashion for reference purposes. If negotiations become lengthy and complex, as they often do, these communications can help you to keep up with progress being made. Understand, until accepted and agreed upon by both parties, statements made during negotiations are for discussion purposes only. In short, neither party will be bound by terms discussed or preliminarily agreed upon.

It is common during negotiations for the parties and their attorneys to participate in joint face to face negotiation sessions. These sessions are also known as 4-way meetings and can be very helpful and productive.

## 9 Tips When Participating in a 4-Way Meeting are:

1. Remain as calm and non-adversarial as possible.
2. Take time to think prior to making agreements.
3. Keep unrelated issues out of the meeting.
4. Bring a copy of your *What Now? Tactical Divorce Plan* with you to use as a reference guide.
5. Be flexible and reasonable.
6. Don't waste time discussing insignificant issues. Remember you are being charged by the hour.
7. Be prepared for the meeting. Bring all of your notes and records with you.
8. Listen to the advice of your attorney.
9. Stay focused on settlement.

## ~~Alternative Dispute Resolution~~

If settlement is not reached through lawyer driven negotiations, there are many alternative methods used to resolve conflict. Explore using alternative dispute resolution (ADR). Alternative dispute resolution is generally less expensive than court intervention. It is also much less adversarial than litigation. Parties involved in ADR maintain greater control over the process. ADR also allows maximum privacy. Two ADR methods are commonly used: mediation and arbitration.

## ~~Mediation~~

With the help of a mediator, parties work through the issues of disagreement to reach a mutually acceptable workable agreement. Mediators generally charge for services on an hourly basis. Mediation is the least adversarial ADR method and should be considered first. In many states mediation is required by the court as part of the divorce process. Many state courts provide mediation services to divorcing parties, often free of charge.

## ~~Arbitration~~

Each side presents their case to a single arbitrator or an arbitration panel. After hearing both sides, the arbitrator(s) render a decision.

Arbitration can be binding, meaning parties are legally bound to abide by the arbitration decision. Arbitration may also be non-binding; parties are not legally bound to accept the decision.

Some do's and don'ts to consider when participating in arbitration or mediation:

### Do's

- Remain calm.
- Keep priorities in focus.
- Be prepared.
- Keep focused on resolution.
- Be reasonable.
- Carefully consider decisions.
- Listen to your attorney's advice.

### Don'ts

- Get caught up in the minutia and lose sight of the big picture.
- Sign an agreement that you are not comfortable with.
- Sign an agreement which you do not understand.
- Agree to terms which do not meet your priority needs.
- Be rude, belittling, or overly emotional.
- Settle for anything to get it over with.

# *Chapter 17*

## *When Amicable Becomes Contentious*

### ~~Knowing When to Switch Gears~~

Generally, every effort is made to settle divorce cases without the necessity of a full-out trial. The divorce process is designed to incorporate aspects of alternative dispute resolution methods such as negotiation, mediation and arbitration in an effort to settle the issues without a full-out protracted trial. In the majority of cases, these and other methods work and the terms and conditions of the divorce are agreed upon by the parties. However in a small percentage of cases, for a variety of reasons, settlement cannot be reached and the case must proceed to trial. If your case does proceed to trial it is imperative to thoroughly prepare legally and emotionally.

### ~~Knowing When it is Time to Go to Trial~~

The bulk of legal fees are accumulated during the negotiations. It is wise to set limitations on the amount of time and money you are willing and able to expend negotiating a settlement. Decide how many hours you are willing to pay for in the negotiation process. When you hit that amount, stop and request to proceed to trial. Advise your attorney of the limit you have set as early in the process as possible.

You have set reasonable goals in your planning. If after several rounds of negotiations, there is still a large gap between your minimal proposal and the offers from your husband, step back and assess the wisdom of continuing settlement negotiations. Meet with your attorney and other team members to weigh the pros and cons of continuing negotiations.

> **Some factors to consider when deciding if proceeding to trial is necessary:**
>
> - If negotiations continue, is there a reasonable probability that settlement will be reached?
> - What is the probable outcome of a trial? Although your attorney will not know the exact outcome, based on local law and custom, the attorney should be able to make a reasonable predication of the outcome.
> - Is the cost of trial justified?

### ~~Preparing for Trial~~

Before your pretrial meeting with your attorney take time to reexamine your wants and needs. Do they still make sense? Are they within reason?

Request a meeting with your attorney at least 30-45 days prior to trial start date. At this meeting be sure to review all documents which will be presented at trial as well as a list of all witnesses. It is imperative to hold this meeting far enough in advance to allow for ordering documents which may be necessary.

Your attorney will schedule at least one trial prep conference with you. In preparing for this meeting develop a punch list of items to discuss. Often people forget certain items during the discussions; put your list in writing so you will not forget. Also be sure to review all documentary evidence with your attorney to ensure all documents are correct and available.

Finally and most importantly, your testimony should be reviewed. If possible, request a copy of the questions prior to the meeting to allow time to prepare well thought out responses. Also be sure to discuss the testimony of your soon to be ex-husband, as well as any witnesses you plan to have called at trial. This review will give you the opportunity to add or delete as necessary.

Be sure your attorney has all information requested. Keep copies of all documents for your own file. If possible, on the day of the trial have your copies handy.

Be sure to tell your attorney of any negative issues which may come to light at trial. Even if you believe the issue is insignificant due to the passage of time or any other reason, tell your attorney anyway. If you think it is an issue that your soon to be ex-husband will either forget or just not bring up, think again. Generally speaking, nothing is off limits during trial. Do not let your attorney be blindsided.

At least a couple of days prior to trial, physically go to the courthouse to check out the parking situation. Go in and get a lay of the land, including the courtroom. If possible, sit in on a trial or proceeding, ideally with the judge who will hear your case. Also find out courthouse rules which will affect you: dress code, possession and use of cell phones. This will go a long way in helping you feel comfortable at the day of the trial.

### ~~Getting Through Trial~~

The actual days of trial will be tough, no way around it. Try your best to remain calm. Arrive early to give yourself time to settle in. Be sure to make alternate arrangements for child care or transportation if necessary. Wear comfortable shoes and clothing.

Some items you should bring are:

1. Pad of paper and pen for taking notes.
2. A small snack such as a granola or protein bar.
3. Tissues.
4. Duplicate copies of documents.

### ~~Giving Testimony~~

When testifying be sure to answer the question asked. While this may seem obvious, many people get off track and ramble. They end up giving more information than is necessary or prudent. You do not want to open the door for your husband's attorney to discover information which may be detrimental. Take a three prong approach: 1) listen closely to the question, 2) pause for 3-5 seconds to process the question, 3) answer the question.

If you do not understand the question ask for it to be rephrased or repeated. And perhaps most importantly; if you do not know the answer to the question, say "I don't know." Do not attempt to make up an answer. Giving the wrong answer could be used by opposing counsel to discredit you.

**Your spouse's testimony:** You will likely disagree or take issue with much of your spouse's testimony. Do not show your disagreement. Gesturing, verbal outbursts and engaging your spouse in a shouting match while he is testifying will only annoy the judge. Keep calm and collected. Emotional outbursts will not help you to gain the sympathy of the judge.

**Working with your attorney during trial:** During testimony your attorney must pay close attention and concentrate. Avoid diverting your attorney's attention by asking questions or making comments. I always provide my clients with paper and pen to jot down notes. I read them when there is a quick break in the action. Write legibly.

**Your personal support network:** On the day of trial it is strongly advised that you do not come to court alone. Bring along a support person. During breaks you may need a shoulder to cry on. You may want to bounce things off someone else as decisions may need to be made. Your support person is another set of eyes and ears who can catch gaps and be sure everything comes out that is supposed to come out.

# Chapter 18

## Redefining Yourself

As little girls, many of us spent hours daydreaming of a time when we would be all grown-up. What kind of a career would we have? Would we have children? And, for most, there is always the Prince Charming in those dreams, the man with whom we would live happily ever after.

In our late teens and 20s we believe we can make our dreams come true, planning and preparing for every role: career woman, wife, mother. Life could really turn out the way we dreamed.

By the time we are in our 30s, if we are blessed enough and put in the right time and effort, we have gotten the momentum and are living the life we dreamed of, the life we carefully created.

Sometimes challenges occur and we are thrown off track. The well crafted life takes an unexpected turn and we are faced with life scenarios never dreamt, and much less planned for. A failed marriage is one of those scenarios. No one dreams of the day their life will shatter and they will be divorced.

When your divorce becomes final you have two choices: 1) spend days, weeks, even years mourning the lost dream, or 2) challenge yourself to recreate your life. Use this time as an opportunity to dream again. Decide who you want to be in your new life. Plan and prepare just as you have in the past. Get rid of the self imposed limitations, and ask yourself, who am I now? Who do I want be? Take the time to figure out your new roles. Redefine yourself.

Begin by looking at all of the other roles you play: mother, daughter, friend, career woman. Are those areas working? What will make those areas even better?

Next, step back and contemplate the life you desire. What are your passions, dreams, aspirations? What does your new life look like? What parts of your life will remain, what parts should be removed and what new parts do you want to include?

What concrete action do you need to take to create the life you envision? List out those steps. Go down the list and take the necessary actions.

Next develop a personal vision statement. Include all of your hopes and dreams, address and conquer your self imposed limitations, and set short term and long term goals.

Finally, but most importantly, make it happen!

## Step Four Summary

Step four is the culmination of all of your hard work in steps 1, 2, and 3. Using your completed *What Now? Tactical Divorce Plan* you have taken control of your situation and gotten through the divorce process in a cohesive manner. You have made well thought out and informed decisions. You are ready to move forward and live the life you desire. Congratulations!

*If you can imagine it, you can achieve it; if you can dream it, you can become it." **William Arthur Ward***

# *What Now? Tactical Divorce Plan Workbook*

## STEP ONE:  LAYING THE FOUNDATION

## My Personal Support Network:

Whenever I need to laugh and relax, _____
(good time friend) is who I call.

_____ (historic friend) has always been there
for me through thick and thin and knows my history.

I can always count on _____ (logical friend) when
I need to process information and make sound, unemotional
decisions.

I can always count on_____ (reality check friend)
to tell me the truth even when it's hard to hear or I don't want to
hear it.

When I am feeling discouraged, _____(cheerleader
friend) will help lift my spirits.

I need to be careful about revealing confidential information to:

_____

_____

_____

_____

_____

_____

## Who Else Needs to Be Told And Why

_____ should be told because

_____

_____

_____

_____ should be told because

_____

_____

_____

_____ should be told because

_____

_____

_____

_____ should be told because

_____

_____

_____

_____ should be told because

_____

_____

_____

_____ should be told because

_____

_____

_____

_____ should be told because

_____

_____

_____

_____ should be told because

_____

_____

_____

# NOTES

_____

_____

_____

_____

_____

_____

_____

_____

_____

_____

_____

_____

_____

_____

_____

## Putting Together My Professional Team

On my team, I need:

☐      Physician

☐      Accountant

☐      Lawyer

☐      Financial Planner

☐      Insurance Agent

☐      Asset Valuator

☐      Therapist/Lifecoach

☐      Other

## Evaluations

### Primary Physician 1:

Name _____

Date of Consultation _____

Initial Impressions _____

_____

_____

_____

_____

Fee Structure _____

Concerns _____

Positives/Negatives _____

_____

_____

_____

_____

## **Primary Physician 2:**

Name _____

Date of Consultation _____

Initial Impressions _____

_____

_____

_____

_____

Fee Structure _____

Concerns _____

Positives/Negatives _____

_____

_____

_____

_____

## Primary Physician 3:

Name _____

Date of Consultation _____

Initial Impressions _____

_____

_____

_____

_____

Fee Structure _____

Concerns _____

Positives/Negatives _____

_____

_____

_____

_____

## Accountant 1:

Name _____

Date of Consultation _____

Initial Impressions _____

_____

_____

_____

_____

Fee Structure _____

Concerns _____

Positives/Negatives _____

_____

_____

_____

_____

## Accountant 2:

Name _____

Date of Consultation _____

Initial Impressions _____

_____

_____

_____

_____

Fee Structure _____

Concerns _____

Positives/Negatives _____

_____

_____

_____

_____

## Accountant 3:

Name _____

Date of Consultation _____

Initial Impressions _____

_____

_____

_____

_____

Fee Structure _____

Concerns _____

Positives/Negatives _____

_____

_____

_____

_____

## Lawyer 1:

Name _____

Date of Consultation _____

Initial Impressions _____

_____

_____

_____

_____

Fee Structure _____

Concerns _____

Positives/Negatives _____

_____

_____

_____

_____

## Lawyer 2:

Name _____

Date of Consultation _____

Initial Impressions _____

_____

_____

_____

_____

Fee Structure _____

Concerns _____

Positives/Negatives _____

_____

_____

_____

_____

## Lawyer 3:

Name _____

Date of Consultation _____

Initial Impressions _____

_____

_____

_____

_____

Fee Structure _____

Concerns _____

Positives/Negatives _____

_____

_____

_____

_____

## Financial Planner 1:

Name _____

Date of Consultation _____

Initial Impressions _____

_____

_____

_____

_____

Fee Structure _____

Concerns _____

Positives/Negatives _____

_____

_____

_____

_____

**Financial Planner 2:**

Name _____

Date of Consultation _____

Initial Impressions _____

_____

_____

_____

_____

Fee Structure _____

Concerns _____

Positives/Negatives _____

_____

_____

_____

_____

## **Financial Planner 3:**

Name _____

Date of Consultation _____

Initial Impressions _____

_____

_____

_____

_____

Fee Structure _____

Concerns _____

Positives/Negatives _____

_____

_____

_____

_____

## Insurance Agent 1:

Name _____

Date of Consultation _____

Initial Impressions _____

_____

_____

_____

_____

Fee Structure _____

Concerns _____

Positives/Negatives _____

_____

_____

_____

_____

## Insurance Agent 2:

Name _____

Date of Consultation _____

Initial Impressions _____

_____

_____

_____

_____

Fee Structure _____

Concerns _____

Positives/Negatives _____

_____

_____

_____

_____

## Insurance Agent 3:

Name _____

Date of Consultation _____

Initial Impressions _____

_____

_____

_____

_____

Fee Structure _____

Concerns _____

Positives/Negatives_____

_____

_____

_____

_____

## Asset Valuator 1:

Name _____

Date of Consultation _____

Initial Impressions _____

_____

_____

_____

_____

Fee Structure _____

Concerns _____

Positives/Negatives _____

_____

_____

_____

_____

## Asset Valuator 2:

Name _____

Date of Consultation _____

Initial Impressions _____

_____

_____

_____

_____

Fee Structure _____

Concerns _____

Positives/Negatives _____

_____

_____

_____

_____

## Asset Valuator 3:

Name _____

Date of Consultation _____

Initial Impressions _____

_____

_____

_____

_____

Fee Structure _____

Concerns _____

Positives/Negatives _____

_____

_____

_____

_____

## Therapist/Life Coach 1:

Name _____

Date of Consultation _____

Initial Impressions _____

_____

_____

_____

_____

Fee Structure _____

Concerns _____

Positives/Negatives _____

_____

_____

_____

_____

## Therapist/Life Coach 2:

Name _____

Date of Consultation _____

Initial Impressions _____

_____

_____

_____

_____

Fee Structure _____

Concerns _____

Positives/Negatives _____

_____

_____

_____

_____

## Therapist/Life Coach 3:

Name _____

Date of Consultation _____

Initial Impressions _____

_____

_____

_____

_____

Fee Structure _____

Concerns _____

Positives/Negatives _____

_____

_____

_____

_____

## **Other 1:**

Name _____

Date of Consultation _____

Initial Impressions _____

_____

_____

_____

_____

Fee Structure _____

Concerns _____

Positives/Negatives _____

_____

_____

_____

_____

## Other 2:

Name _____

Date of Consultation _____

Initial Impressions _____

_____

_____

_____

_____

Fee Structure _____

Concerns _____

Positives/Negatives _____

_____

_____

_____

_____

## Other 3:

Name _____

Date of Consultation _____

Initial Impressions _____

_____

_____

_____

_____

Fee Structure _____

Concerns _____

Positives/Negatives _____

_____

_____

_____

_____

## My Professional Team

### Primary Physician:

Name _____

Address _____

Telephone _____

Email _____

### Accountant:

Name _____

Address _____

Telephone _____

Email _____

### Lawyer:

Name _____

Address _____

Telephone _____

Email _____

## Financial Planner:

Name ——————————————————————

Address ——————————————————————

Telephone ——————————————————————

Email ——————————————————————

## Insurance Agent:

Name——————————————————————

Address ——————————————————————

Telephone ——————————————————————

Email ——————————————————————

## Assset Valuator:

Name ——————————————————————

Address ——————————————————————

Telephone ——————————————————————

Email ——————————————————————

## Therapist/Life Coach:

Name _____

Address _____

Telephone _____

Email _____

## Other:

Name _____

Address _____

Telephone _____

Email _____

Address _____

Telephone _____

Email _____

## STEP TWO:  UNDERSTANDING THE PRESENT

## Financial

Day-to-day financial management

### Your Personal Income

Consistent Income:

| | |
|---|---|
| Monthly net salary | $ _____ |
| Monthly net pension income | $ _____ |
| Social Security income | $ _____ |
| Asset produced income | $ _____ |
| Variable income | $ _____ |
| Self-employment income | $ _____ |
| Partnership/ ownership Draw | $ _____ |
| Tips | $ _____ |
| Commissions and bonuses | $ _____ |
| Passive and residual income | $ _____ |
| **Your Total Net Monthly Income** | $ _____ |

### Your Spouse's Income

Consistent Income:

| | |
|---|---|
| Monthly net salary | $ _____ |
| Monthly net pension income | $ _____ |
| Social Security income | $ _____ |
| Asset produced income | $ _____ |
| Variable income | $ _____ |

Self-employment income                                  $ _____

Partnership/ ownership Draw                         $ _____

Tips                                                             $ _____

Commissions and bonuses                            $ _____

Passive and residual income                         $ _____

**Your Spouse's Total Net Monthly Income** $ _____


**Total  Household Net Monthly Income**    $ _____

## Household Expenses

### Variable expenses:

| | |
|---|---|
| Heating fuel | $ _____ |
| Electric | $ _____ |
| Water | $ _____ |
| Telephone | $ _____ |
| Trash collection | $ _____ |
| Home maintenance | $ _____ |
| Cable Television | $ _____ |
| Food | $ _____ |
| Clothing | $ _____ |
| Public transportation | $ _____ |
| Auto gas/oil | $ _____ |
| Personal grooming | $ _____ |
| Pet cost | $ _____ |
| Out of pocket medical | $ _____ |
| Organization dues | $ _____ |
| Charitable contributions | $ _____ |
| Credit card payments | $ _____ |
| Other | $ _____ |
| **Total variable expenses:** | $ _____ |

## Fixed expenses:

Mortgage(s)        $ _____

Rent        $ _____

Property taxes        $ _____

Life insurance premiums        $ _____

Health insurance premiums        $ _____

Long term health care insurance premiums        $ _____

Disability insurance premiums        $ _____

Auto insurance premiums        $ _____

Auto loan        $ _____

Other        $ _____

**Total fixed expenses:**        $ _____

Once all expenses have been calculated, add 10%-20% to the final expense total in contemplation of cost of living increases, unexpected, and miscellaneous expenses.

*income – expenses = monthly personal/household operating cost*

## Total Monthly Personal Household Operating Cost        $ _____

*What Now? Divorce Planning*

## Assets and Liabilities

## Joint Intangible Assets

| Asset | Valuation method | Value | Lien/Loan | Equity |
|-------|-----------------|-------|-----------|--------|
|       |                 |       |           |        |
|       |                 |       |           |        |
|       |                 |       |           |        |
|       |                 |       |           |        |
|       |                 |       |           |        |
|       |                 |       |           |        |
|       |                 |       |           |        |
|       |                 |       |           |        |
|       |                 |       |           |        |
|       |                 |       |           |        |
|       |                 |       |           |        |
|       |                 |       |           |        |

**Total Value of Joint Intangible Assets:** $ _____

## My Intangible Assets

| Asset | Valuation method | Value | Lien/Loan | Equity |
|---|---|---|---|---|
| | | | | |

**Total Value of My Intangible Assets:** $ _____

**Total Value of All Intangible Assets:** $ _____

163

# Joint Tangible Assets

| Asset | Valuation method | Value | Lien/Loan | Equity |
|---|---|---|---|---|
|  |  |  |  |  |
|  |  |  |  |  |
|  |  |  |  |  |
|  |  |  |  |  |
|  |  |  |  |  |
|  |  |  |  |  |
|  |  |  |  |  |
|  |  |  |  |  |
|  |  |  |  |  |
|  |  |  |  |  |
|  |  |  |  |  |

**Total Value of Joint Tangible Assets:**   $ _____

## My Tangible Assets

| Asset | Valuation method | Value | Lien/Loan | Equity |
|---|---|---|---|---|
| | | | | |

**Total Value of My Tangible Assets:**    $ _____

**Total Value of All Tangible Assets:**    $ _____

## Joint Income Producing Assets

Asset          Valuation method          Value          Lien/Loan          Equity

_____

_____

_____

_____

_____

_____

_____

_____

_____

_____

_____

_____

_____

_____

_____

_____

**Total Value of Joint Inc. Producing Assets:**   $ _____

## My Income Producing Assets

| Asset | Valuation method | Value | Lien/Loan | Equity |
|-------|------------------|-------|-----------|--------|
| | | | | |
| | | | | |
| | | | | |
| | | | | |
| | | | | |
| | | | | |
| | | | | |
| | | | | |
| | | | | |
| | | | | |
| | | | | |
| | | | | |

**Total Value of My Income Producing Assets:** $ _____

**Total Value of All Income Producing Assets:** $ _____

## Joint Liabilities

Creditor                Original Debt                Balance Due

_____

_____

_____

_____

_____

_____

_____

_____

_____

_____

_____

_____

_____

**Total Joint Liability:**                $ _____

## My Individual Liabilities

| Creditor | Original Debt | Balance Due |
|----------|---------------|-------------|
|          |               |             |

**Total My Individual Liability:**    $ _____

**Total of All Liabilities:**    $ _____

## Legal Matters
## Pending Civil Suits

| Case Name | Case Number | Status |
|-----------|-------------|--------|
| | | |
| | | |
| | | |
| | | |
| | | |
| | | |
| | | |
| | | |
| | | |
| | | |
| | | |
| | | |

## Outstanding Judgments

Plaintiff                    Date of Judgment          Balance Due

_____

_____

_____

_____

_____

_____

_____

_____

_____

_____

_____

_____

## Health

## Existing known Medical conditions

Condition          Medication/              Treating Physician
                   Treatment

_____

_____

_____

_____

_____

_____

_____

_____

_____

_____

_____

_____

## STEP THREE

## MY DAY TO DAY FINANCIAL NEEDS

Total projected post divorce
expenses per month:                    $ _____

My projected post divorce
net employment income:               $ _____

The presumptive child support:    $ _____

My projected after tax alimony:    $ _____

Total projected monthly income:  $ _____

I am therefore able to maintain (or not maintain) my projected monthly household expenses.

To be in a financially healthy position, I need to consider:

_____

_____

_____

_____

_____

_____

## Debt Payment Plan

| Creditor | Amount of Debt | Current Pymts |
|----------|----------------|---------------|
| | | |

## Insurance Coverage I Need

☐    Life

☐    Health

☐    Disability

☐    Long Term Care

☐    Auto

☐    Other

In the event of the death or disability of _____,
I will be able to continue to care for myself and my children financially because the following insurances are in place:

☐     Life Insurance

☐     Disability Insurance

I also have the following contingent savings plan in place:

_____

_____

_____

_____

## Assets Division

Prioritized list of assets I wish to retain:

_____

_____

_____

_____

_____

_____

_____

_____

_____

_____

_____

_____

_____

_____

_____

## Debts I Am Willing To Assume

Creditor                  Amount of Debt                  Current Pymts

_____

_____

_____

_____

_____

_____

_____

_____

_____

_____

_____

_____

_____

_____

## Debts I Am Not Willing To Assume

Creditor                Amount of Debt                Current Pymts

_____

_____

_____

_____

_____

_____

_____

_____

_____

_____

_____

_____

_____

## Jumpstarting My New Life

In order to jumpstart my new life, it would be beneficial for me to:

_____

_____

_____

_____

_____

_____

I can best accomplish this by:

_____

_____

_____

_____

_____

_____

The cost of doing so is $_____

## Children's Expenses

For each child, complete the following worksheet:

Name of Child: _____

| Expense | Average Annual Expenditure |
|---|---|
| Unreimbursed medical cost | $ _____ |
| Unreimbursed medical supplies | $ _____ |
| Unreimbursed orthodontic care | $ _____ |
| Unreimbursed ophthalmic care/supplies | $ _____ |
| Sports | $ _____ |
| Lessons | $ _____ |
| Tutoring | $ _____ |
| Summer camps | $ _____ |
| School lunches | $ _____ |
| School supplies | $ _____ |
| After school programs | $ _____ |
| School field trips | $ _____ |
| Clothing | $ _____ |
| Religious education | $ _____ |
| Religious activities | $ _____ |
| Memberships | $ _____ |
| Entertainment | $ _____ |
| Gifts for friends | $ _____ |
| Transportation | $ _____ |

Grooming                      $ _____

Auto Insurance                $ _____

Other                         $ _____

Total Annual Expenditure      $ _____

## Parental Access Plans

Fill in the current family schedule.

### Current Family Activity Calendar

| | Mon | Tues | Wed | Thurs | Fri | Sat | Sun |
|---|---|---|---|---|---|---|---|
| Week 1 | | | | | | | |
| Week 2 | | | | | | | |
| Week 3 | | | | | | | |
| Week 4 | | | | | | | |

Look at the sample guides and create a Parenting Plan that works for your family. Remember, these are just sample guides. Create a Plan specific for your family's needs.

### Parental Access Plan

| | Mon | Tues | Wed | Thurs | Fri | Sat | Sun |
|---|---|---|---|---|---|---|---|
| Week 1 | | | | | | | |
| Week 2 | | | | | | | |
| Week 3 | | | | | | | |
| Week 4 | | | | | | | |

## Parental Access Plan

| | Mon | Tues | Wed | Thurs | Fri | Sat | Sun |
|---|---|---|---|---|---|---|---|
| Week 1 | | | | | | | |
| Week 2 | | | | | | | |
| Week 3 | | | | | | | |
| Week 4 | | | | | | | |

## Parental Access Plan

| | Mon | Tues | Wed | Thurs | Fri | Sat | Sun |
|---|---|---|---|---|---|---|---|
| Week 1 | | | | | | | |
| Week 2 | | | | | | | |
| Week 3 | | | | | | | |
| Week 4 | | | | | | | |

## Parental Access Plan

| | Mon | Tues | Wed | Thurs | Fri | Sat | Sun |
|---|---|---|---|---|---|---|---|
| Week 1 | | | | | | | |
| Week 2 | | | | | | | |
| Week 3 | | | | | | | |
| Week 4 | | | | | | | |

# STEP FOUR

## PUTTING YOUR PLAN INTO PLACE

### Keeping Track of Professional Fees

### Contact With Lawyer Log

| Date | Activity | Time Spent |
|------|----------|------------|
|      |          |            |
|      |          |            |
|      |          |            |
|      |          |            |
|      |          |            |
|      |          |            |
|      |          |            |
|      |          |            |
|      |          |            |
|      |          |            |

## Contact With Lawyer Log, con't.

Date             Activity                                    Time Spent

_____

_____

_____

_____

_____

_____

_____

_____

_____

_____

_____

_____

_____

_____

## Contact With Lawyer Log, con't.

Date            Activity                                Time Spent

_____

_____

_____

_____

_____

_____

_____

_____

_____

_____

_____

_____

_____

_____

## Contact With Accountant

Date            Activity                                Time Spent

_____

_____

_____

_____

_____

_____

_____

_____

_____

_____

_____

_____

_____

_____

## Contact With Accountant Log, con't.

Date          Activity                                  Time Spent

_____

_____

_____

_____

_____

_____

_____

_____

_____

_____

_____

_____

_____

## Contact With Financial Planner/Advisor Log

Date                Activity                                    Time Spent

_____

_____

_____

_____

_____

_____

_____

_____

_____

_____

_____

_____

## Contact With Financial Planner/Advisor Log, Con't.

Date             Activity                                    Time Spent

_____

_____

_____

_____

_____

_____

_____

_____

_____

_____

_____

_____

_____

## Document Log

Date          Document                    Given To

_____

_____

_____

_____

_____

_____

_____

_____

_____

_____

_____

_____

_____

_____

## Document Log, Con't.

Date                Document                                    Given To

_____

_____

_____

_____

_____

_____

_____

_____

_____

_____

_____

_____

_____

_____

## Document Log, Con't.

Date                 Document                        Given To

_____

_____

_____

_____

_____

_____

_____

_____

_____

_____

_____

_____

_____

_____

## Trial Preparation

## Meeting Notes

_____

_____

_____

_____

_____

_____

_____

_____

_____

_____

_____

_____

_____

_____

_____

_____

_____

_____

_____

_____

_____

_____

_____

_____

_____

_____

_____

_____

_____

_____

# Issues to be Discussed at Pretrial Meeting

## Documents to Gather for Trial

_____

_____

_____

_____

_____

_____

_____

_____

_____

_____

_____

_____

_____

_____

_____

# Witness List

_____

_____

_____

_____

_____

_____

_____

_____

_____

_____

_____

_____

_____

_____

_____

## My Personal Vision Statement

Read this vision statement at least 3 times per day for 1 week; then read it at least once per day.

In the beginning of the divorce process I believed I was _____

_____

_____.

I feared _____

_____

_____.

but now that the process is complete, I realize that my fears were

_____.

Although it has been painful and stressful, I have learned _____

_____

_____.

In the past, I have harbored some limiting beliefs about myself. I believed _____

and _____

and _____.

I am ready to disregard these limiting beliefs that have held me back from achieving all that I desire.

I now realize that I am _____

_____

and have many great attributes.

My three greatest attributes are _____

and _____

and _____.

In my role as _____ I have proven that I have what it takes to be successful.

In my role as _____ I have given my all and my effort has paid off.

And, in my role as _____I have found great pleausure.

_____ gives me the greatest joy, and I am happiest when _____.

Have achieved success and found joy and pleasure, I am now ready to move forward and create the life I deserve.

# NOTES

_____

_____

_____

_____

_____

_____

_____

_____

_____

_____

_____

_____

_____

_____

# NOTES

# NOTES

# NOTES

_____

_____

_____

_____

_____

_____

_____

_____

_____

_____

_____

_____

_____

_____

# *Acknowledgements*

There have been so many people who knowingly or unknowingly have provided support and encouragement in writing this book. A special thanks to:

Amy Doughten, who once again did a phenomenal layout and design job.

Jeff Baughn, my wonderful editor.

My circle of friends who have helped me navigate through the tough times and have shared my joy in the good times.

My daughter Brittany, who always sees the glass as half full and always reminds me to keep filling it up.

My parents William and Ella Giles, without whom so much in my life would not be possible.

Finally, but most significantly, I thank God, without whom nothing in my life  would be possible.

# Index

# H

housing 68

# I

income
  passive 32
Income 31
income producing assets 32
Income producing assets 34
insurance
  auto 57, 70
  coverage during divorce 57
  coverage post divorce 58
  disability 57, 72
  health 57
  life 57, 70, 71
  long term care 57
  medical 49, 70
  post-divorce 49
intangible assets 34

# J

Jewelry
  valuating 38
Joint legal and physical custody 90
Joint legal custody 89

# L

Laws
  divorce law 11
  state specific 11
Lawsuits, Judgments, and Liens 44
  loans 46
  title search 45
Liabilities 40
liens 44
  property 45
Life coach 22
loans 46
  co-signed 46

# M

# N

# P

# T

# V

# W

Made in the USA
San Bernardino, CA
20 November 2018